Edward Elgar: the record of a friendship

Facing photograph. Miss Rosa Burley
taken in Rome about 1903

Photograph overleaf. Sir Edward Elgar
at the piano in the music room at
'The Mount' Malvern

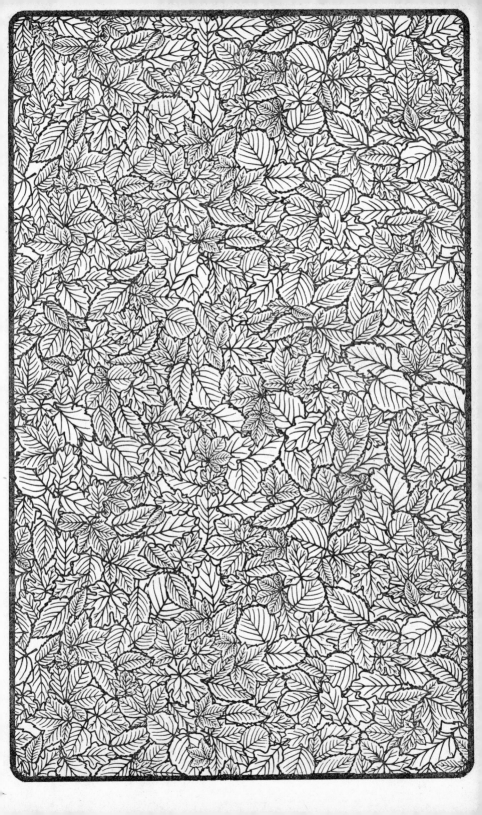

EDWARD ELGAR

the record
of a friendship

by
ROSA BURLEY
and
FRANK C. CARRUTHERS

BARRIE & JENKINS
LONDON

© 1972 by Mrs I. M. Fresson
All rights reserved
First published 1972 by
BARRIE & JENKINS LTD
2 Clement's Inn, London WC2
Printed in Great Britain by
W & J Mackay Limited, Chatham

ISBN 0 214 65410 9

PUBLISHER'S NOTE

The typescript of this book was completed by 1948. Miss Burley died in 1951 and Mr Carruthers in 1958 when the typescript came into the possession of the present owner of the copyright, who decided not to offer it for publication during the lifetime of Elgar's daughter, Mrs Elgar-Blake.

The original typescript is somewhat longer than the present printed version since, for the period after Miss Burley went abroad in 1906, the authors included much biographical material about Elgar, which is available elsewhere, and on which Miss Burley had no first-hand evidence to add to the known facts. With the agreement of the owner of the copyright such passages have been omitted, and the chapters on the later years limited to those periods and occasions when Miss Burley was able to be in personal contact with Elgar.

CONTENTS

Edward Elgar: the record of a friendship

Foreword

The pages that follow are the fruit of a true collaboration since, while the memories of Edward Elgar which formed the starting point are those of Miss Burley, practically all the actual writing and a certain amount of research have been contributed by Mr Carruthers.

The aim of the book is to describe Elgar as he appeared to perhaps the only person, other than Lady Elgar and his daughter, Carice (Mrs Elgar-Blake), who was in daily contact with him from the year 1891 when, almost completely unknown, he was teaching the violin in Malvern, till 1904 when he left the district. To such an observer he was bound to present a picture very different from that seen by admirers who did not meet him till he was famous and who, deceived by the mask which in self-defence he had learned by then to adopt and by their own veneration for the musician, were often completely blind to the character of the man.

Unfortunately the popular conception of Elgar's character today seems to be based very largely on the misconceptions of these admirers and we are almost asked to accept him as a lovable, if sometimes rather perverse, country gentleman who somehow found time in the intervals between playing golf, getting himself knighted, taking long walks over the Malvern Hills, dining with Edward VII, sitting in various suitable London clubs and dressing like an elderly colonel, to become one of our greatest composers.

Miss Burley, who really knew the Elgars intimately throughout the period of Edward Elgar's greatest activity as a composer, is anxious to correct this false impression and the object
of the present writers is to describe the man as she knew him.
She did not by any means see his character as that of a hero but
neither does she—nor her collaborator—wish to belittle those
qualities in him which were truly great. The aim indeed is to
approach truth as nearly as our faulty human perception will
allow.

The many passages in the book which take the form of
actual personal reminiscence and are cast in the first person
singular, are Miss Burley's.

ROSA C. BURLEY
FRANK C. CARRUTHERS

1

Prelude: The School

It was in the spring of 1891 that I first met Edward Elgar and formed a friendship that was to affect my whole life. The chain of circumstances leading to that meeting was extraordinarily fortuitous. For some time I had been looking for a finishing school for girls and it happened that, of the schools which were changing hands, the one which most appealed to me, and which I ultimately took, was in Great Malvern.

The Mount, as it was called, was a largish stucco house with that look of a Swiss chalet so much beloved by Victorian architects. It had good rooms, stood in its own pleasant grounds with a large garden at the back, and commanded from the windows which looked across this garden a magnificent view of the Malvern Hills. The Mount is now a house of Malvern Girls' College and may be seen by anyone who cares to stroll down Albert Road. Except for the addition of an external iron staircase, it still looks much as it did in 1891.

The school had been carried on for many years by three elderly women who were now retiring. It was advertised as being 'prepared to receive young ladies, the daughters of gentlemen'. Today we should call them more briefly, and, as I think, sensibly, 'girls', the older phrase having suffered a social decline. The change of name is of interest to me, indicating, as it does, a change of attitude to the whole subject of the educa-tion of women. In this I played some part; indeed it was my anxiety to participate in the new movement that led me to take a school of my own.

Although I was very young at the time, I had gained a certain amount of experience through teaching at Miss Smith's school in Sussex Square, Brighton. Sussex Square was the nursery of much educational development in those days for it contained two other schools, one aristocratic and exclusive kept by the Miss Prangleys, representing the type that was passing, and another that was to achieve fame when later it was moved to Roedean. There was considerable and not always very good-natured rivalry amongst the three.

The development in the education of girls which took place during the later eighties was of course due to changes in the life for which that education had to prepare them. The school for the daughters of gentlemen belonged to a time when life had a certain leisured dignity and when manners and deport-ment were of importance to those about to take a place in society. Girls were therefore taught many things which today would arouse derision. They had to learn how to come into, and leave, a room, how to sit gracefully on a chair and much else of a similar kind. To lounge or sprawl was unforgivable. All walks outside the school grounds were taken in orderly crocodile formation with governesses at the tail.

With the wider horizons that were opening out for women it was evident that new methods were due. I myself did not sub-scribe to what was at first the most widely proclaimed of these, namely that girls should be educated exactly as boys. With the first advent of games-mistresses, cricket, hockey, lacrosse and Swedish drill, the girls developed their muscles but the sub-sequent results were often less desirable. The hide-bound tradi-tions of the older schools were certainly obsolete but I felt that the emancipation of women would not be brought about by a disregard of the psychological and physical difference between the sexes. I wanted girls to be given a more liberal view of life than was then usual and I wanted them particularly to cultivate an appreciation of the arts, especially of the great and neglected art of music. When the opportunity to take The Mount presented itself, therefore, I felt that my visions of a school that should be something as yet undreamt of by others were at last to take shape. This youthful enthusiasm was encouraged by my first sight of Malvern. I had never been in that part of England before and its beauty enchanted me. I looked at the string of villages laced round the foot of the whale-back of hills, at the winding Severn with its rich green valley and I felt that here was the ideal place in which girls might grow up to love beauty.

The ladies who kept The Mount were of interest to me if only for the difference of their outlook from mine and for their complete disregard and ignorance of the new movements which were arising. None of them was in any modern sense 'educated'. Miss Sarah and Miss Sophie were sisters. Miss Mary, their chief of staff, was a friend. Miss Mary was not a very attractive woman nor was she particularly efficient in her management of the curriculum. She suffered from what were described as bilious attacks and periodically was prostrated for days on end with results that were unfortunate for school discipline. What caused these bilious attacks was never disclosed, but many years later when a summer house which had rotted badly was removed from the garden an enormous number of whisky bottles was discovered under the floor.

The two sisters, Miss Sarah and Miss Sophie, were completely unlike one another. Miss Sophie was unassuming and rather undistinguished but Miss Sarah, who was the leading spirit of the trinity, was simply terrific. She was not a woman of great culture or even of much intelligence but she had instinctively developed and followed a few simple rules for achieving success which had proved highly efficacious. The first of these was that a high-class school must be placed in the right kind of district. She had therefore migrated from Wolverhampton, where she had begun, to Malvern. The choice had been dictated by sound strategy. At the time of her move there was growing amongst parents a feeling that children were the better for being brought up in healthy and beautiful surroundings. These Malvern offered in full measure and for Miss Sarah it possessed the additional attraction that its situation gave her the chance to draw on five large West Midland towns not only for her pupils but for the visiting masters and mistresses who provided most of the instruction.

Miss Sarah's second rule, again of course purely instinctive, was that, since the parents of a child always tended to be anxious about her, it was as well to undertake actively to protect her from something. And the danger from which Miss Sarah undertook to protect her pupils was what she grandly described as 'the errors of Rome.' It was in this matter that she showed herself a true child of her generation for her firmly-held and perfectly sincere religious beliefs, so far from being a handicap, became a business asset of the first order. She had in her youth come under the influence of a member (not the famous novelist) of the Baring-Gould family. Whatever the Reverend Mr Baring-Gould might have thought of his responsibility, he had, so she always said, 'formed her mind.' His views were quoted on all occasions of doubt and his splendid double-barrelled name was a moral support on which she never relied in vain.

Whether her violently Evangelical views genuinely represented, and were not a distortion, of his teaching I do not know. What is certain is that by working on their fears of Rome she was able to convince the parents of her pupils that The Mount was a fortress into which the insidious Catholic doctrines could never penetrate. I must admit that when on the change of ownership these parents came to see me they seemed more concerned with the food and physical health of their daughters than with the errors of Rome but no doubt they were impressed by the evidence of a high moral tone. In explaining her views to me she struck a slightly more materialistic note.

'You see, my d'yah,' she said, 'there are very few low-church schools of a good class in the country and parents of strict views have difficulty in finding one where the teaching is *sound*.'

Now Malvern was in those days a stronghold of Low Church practice and therefore provided exactly the setting in which Miss Sarah's appeal could be best exploited. One may add in parenthesis that, for all its beauty, it was, socially very dull, or seemed so to me after Brighton. Completely Victorian, it was a favourite resort of wealthy Quakers and prosperous business people from the Midlands and North who lived there quietly but in extreme comfort. Malvern's great days had been earlier when the famous Dr Gully had cured people's bodies at the Hydro while the no less famous Dr Fiske had wrestled for their souls from the pulpit of the Priory, but the tradition lived on. The only place of public amusement was the Assembly Rooms at which a few dances and concerts were given and, even more rarely, theatrical performances by touring companies on their way to Cheltenham. Donkeys which roamed over the hills by St Ann's Well could be hired and there were walks and drives into the surrounding country. And occasionally in the streets would be heard the sound of a small German band which played discreetly and gave a slightly wistful air of gaiety.

The very healthiness of Malvern attracted the elderly.

'Round about the Malvern Hill
A man may live as long as he will,'

runs the old rhyme and I felt that I could believe it. I was told that in one road alone there were ninety old ladies whose combined years greatly exceeded the age of the earth as computed by Archbishop Usher. Retired clergymen also abounded. One of them, indeed, a dear doddering old gentleman with a long white beard, came to The Mount once a week during Miss Sarah's reign to give the girls what they themselves described as pi-talks. He called the class his garden of flowers. The girls listened quietly but had been known to giggle. . . . Even the church that the school attended had been built in memory of a noted Evangelical divine and as a protest against the ritualistic practices that were creeping into the worship at the Priory.

The third rule on which the success of The Mount had been founded was that the head of the establishment must be a splendid and impressive figure and this requirement Miss Sarah herself fulfilled in no uncertain manner. In person she was tall with markedly horse-like features resembling George Eliot's. In addition she had a majesty of presence and of utterance which overwhelmed all opposition. It overwhelmed her pupils, it overwhelmed their parents and it nearly overwhelmed me during the term which she spent in initiating me into the routine of the school.

'My d'yah,' she would say in her magnificent booming voice, when I had tentatively offered some suggestion of which she did not approve, 'do you think this *wise*?' It took a good deal of courage to maintain that one did.

This term of joint management was a severe trial to us both on account of the divergence of our views on practically all subjects. In our discussions Miss Sarah had the advantage of age and authority and of being, as I afterwards discovered, entirely right within the limits of her own conception of educational success. The trouble was that our aims were entirely different and that, as we had not defined them, she was bound to think me unduly idealistic, and I to think her unduly concerned with mere money-making. I had yet to appreciate the extent to which money-making is necessary in the pursuit of ideals.

During this term we usually arranged the general policy of the school over breakfast and it was then that she treated me to the views on religion and art which formed the basis of her educational philosophy. I had not realized, when taking the school, the full ferocity of her Evangelical ardour and its first impact came as a shock. In our preliminary discussions she had, it is true, mentioned the strictly Low-Church principles on which the teaching of the school was based but, having myself always been associated with moderate churchmanship, I thought the matter was of no great consequence and paid little attention. There were other questions of more pressing importance. The first intimation I received of the violence of her feelings was when she referred to Newman's *Apologia*. Had the *Apologia* been some monstrous piece of pornography she could not have spoken of it with greater abhorrence. It was 'a most dreadful book' which was doing untold harm to the Church, a menace to the young and indeed the thin end of the wedge of Roman Catholic influence.

What she would have said had she known that her successor was to be closely associated with the musical setting of a poem by this same hated writer one hardly dares to think. It may be, however, that she was indifferent to such ironies since her own sister, Miss Sophie, as I learned later, had become a Catholic. I found that Miss Sophie was not allowed to attend the Catholic church in Malvern but used to steal away to Worcester for Mass every Sunday morning.

From the subject of religion it was a relief to turn to Miss Sarah's views on art, which in a school so largely concerned with the more social accomplishments could not be wholly ignored. The girls learned drawing from a little man who came from Cheltenham and gave them water-colours to copy. Dancing was taught by a member of the accomplished D'Egville family, a relative of the D'Egville who had trained Edmund Kean, and of Taglioni. The subject of music, however, offered certain difficulties. When I took over, lessons in both pianoforte and violin were being given. I myself was rather more interested in the latter which I had studied for a short time with the father of Leo Stern. Miss Sarah had other views which were amusingly typical of her outlook and which she imparted to me with oracular gravity.

She made the strictly practical point that the piano had the advantage of requiring no accompaniment, whereas the violin was useless by itself (which I could believe, since the Bach Chaconne and other such works would naturally be outside the range of the young ladies), and wound up with a piece of evidently well-considered advice.

'I think, my d'yah,' she said, 'I would not *encourage* the violin. You see p'yahnos' (she had acquired this pronunciation from the mistress who taught the instrument) 'are now so much improved that there is no *need* for the violin.'

Having made this aesthetic point she added what was for her the deciding consideration.

'Moreover it doesn't pay.'

In this, as I found later, she was only too right. But at the time I could not believe that merely commercial considerations should be allowed to interfere with the teaching of what I felt to be the finest of all instruments and I was not to be deflected from my interest.

One morning when this question of rival merits had been under discussion she opened a letter and, passing it to me, said, 'That, d'yah, is from the violin master.'

I gathered that this young man, who came originally from the eight-miles distant city of Worcester, had tried his fortune in London and, having failed, was shortly settling in Malvern to resume a local teaching connection. It appeared that he had visited The Mount once a week from London.

I was not interested. I had seem so many such letters and had coped with so many problems of administration that I only glanced at the signature which was written in a bold and original hand.

It was 'Edward Elgar'.

The name meant nothing to me whatever. What caught my attention was the character of the writing.

2

The Violin Master

My first meeting with the violin master happened rather oddly and was delayed until a good many weeks after the beginning of term. I had decided to make no alterations in the management of The Mount until I had accustomed myself thoroughly to its working and, as Miss Sarah was staying with me for a time to ease the change-over, the school could be allowed to run on its own momentum, leaving me free to observe and to plan such improvements as I thought desirable. I did not meet all the visiting staff at the outset and, as Mr Elgar, who was still living in London, only arrived in the afternoons when Miss Sarah was lying down, and therefore unable to introduce us, he remained for some time the one person connected with the school whom I had never seen.

It will be appreciated of course that in 1891 there was absolutely nothing to indicate to me that he was anything more than a rather provincial young man who came every week to give violin lessons. His *Froissart* overture had, it is true, been produced at the Worcester Festival of the previous year but it had failed to attract much attention even locally. Hardly anyone in Malvern—certainly no one whom I met—had the slightest suspicion that he was a man of outstanding talent, let alone genius.

Nor could this fact be guessed from the standard of musical work in the school. It was evident that Miss Sarah in discourag-

ing the violin had also discouraged the violin master, for there
was no one who played even moderately well. The pianists, too,
who might have produced the stimulus of rivalry, were no
better. It was the practice, I found, to hold weekly musical
evenings at which the girls played or sang the pieces they had
been studying. The first of these evenings produced no performance—not even that of the resident pianoforte mistress—
which had the slightest musical value. After the school at
Brighton, where the teaching of music had been taken very
seriously and where the girls had had the opportunity of hearing and studying the work of every prominent artist of the day,
it was a shock to be faced with the stumbling efforts of children
who could do nothing themselves, and had clearly never heard
a really competent performance by anyone else.

I had, moreover, so much to occupy my attention in these
early days of my new venture that a visiting master easily
escaped any particular notice. There were parents to meet, calls
to return and, in any spare time I could find, one of the loveliest
districts in England to explore. It was good after some of the
calls—such as that, for instance, which had to be made on the
owner of the rival school, a stiff affair indeed—to climb the
Worcestershire Beacon and find that by merely turning my head
I could see the cathedrals of Hereford, Worcester and Gloucester
at my feet. The Malvern Hills are a straight range running from
north to south and parallel with the Severn which flows about
four miles to the east. Between the hills and the river is an
immense tract of country known as the Welland Common over
which the girls used to ride. And on the Welsh side of the hills
are numberless villages which even today are completely un-
spoiled. Often I was glad to forget the school and all its works
in the pleasure of discovering new walks through this delightful
countryside.

Still, some few facts about Mr Elgar had filtered through to
me and they were not wholly reassuring. From various sources
I had learned that he was not always good-tempered and that

in consequence the girls were afraid of him. Thus it was the custom for each pupil at the end of her lesson to telegraph the state of the emotional atmosphere to her successor and there was one child who enraged him to such an extent that the others had begged that she might be placed last on the list in order to prevent her from making things impossible for them. And then there was the affair of the metronome. . . .

In those days it was generally accepted that a chaperone or 'dragon' must always be present during the private lessons given by masters. This convention was no doubt based on a belief that the girls needed protection from the men but my own feeling was that the need was the other way round. In any case, however, the dragon was useful to the school management as a liaison-officer and reporter of progress.

One afternoon some months before I took the school it chanced that the violin lesson was watched by a dragon who was herself something of a music-teacher. She was the kind of teacher, not unknown today, whose whole musical outlook was bounded by the more rudimentary technical rules—the kind of teacher who stops a lesson in the middle of a bar because the hour is up—and she used a metronome. On this particular afternoon the pupil had given the exigencies of a difficult tempo as an excuse for faulty bowing, whereupon Mr Elgar had exclaimed, 'Oh never mind the time. Get the bowing right.' On hearing this the dragon had been roused to frenzy. Clearly the young man knew nothing about the theory of music and must be taught. At the next lesson, therefore, she produced her metronome and explained its use. Mr Elgar's reaction was unexpected. Scorching the metronome with the kind of look that the mace must have received from Cromwell, he exclaimed, 'Take the thing away!'

Beyond this I knew nothing and I doubt if Miss Sarah knew much more. She moved in a very narrow circle, visited and entertained hardly at all and was almost certainly unaware that her violin master was the composer of an overture which had been played at the Worcester Festival. Had she known this indeed it would have meant nothing to her since, for all her dignity she was a relatively uncultured woman and was probably incapable of realizing that he was anything more than a young man who taught the violin. I was therefore completely unprepared for the circumstances of our first meeting.

In a school containing eleven pianos, on each of which someone is practising one of the minor classics, it takes something rather arresting to catch the ear of the suffering listener. One afternoon, however, when the violin master was in attendance, I heard sounds coming from the music-room which made me pause and listen. Apparently waiting for a pupil, who was lingering upstairs in order to shorten the time of tribulation, he was happily playing the piano and—as I should guess in the light of later knowledge—hoping that she would never turn up.

What he was playing I did not know and, as he had probably never played it before, this was not really surprising, but it had a quality that was unmistakable. Descriptions of the effect produced by music are notoriously unsuccessful and perhaps the only thing to be said is that what I heard that afternoon seemed to detach itself from the mill of sound in the school with a suddenness and strangeness that I have never forgotten. Hardly able to wait for the first full close I pushed open the door and went in.

A tall slight young man with a pale face and dark eyes rose hastily and rather awkwardly from the piano and stood scowling at me. Clearly the interruption was not welcome. Feeling rather chilled, I told him my name and said that I hoped his pupils were working satisfactorily. This elicited some sort of mumbled reply which struck me as, if anything, more hostile than his silence. He then stood blinking at me for what seemed a very long time until my struggle to think of some further contribution to this not very promising conversation was mercifully interrupted by the arrival of the pupil and her dragon, a

German governess who always crocheted throughout the lesson. Somewhat deflated, I withdrew.

Many months later he gave me an explanation. It appeared that by some mischance he had never learned of the school's change of ownership and that in consequence my name meant nothing to him. He took me, I think, for another of the hated dragons and probably anticipated, if not a second metronome, some further source of exasperation. Shortly afterwards the matter was straightened out when Mr D'Egville, meeting him in Worcester, asked him how he liked the new headmistress at The Mount. The next time that Mr Elgar visited the school he was more friendly and when he found that, so far from sharing Miss Sarah's view of the violin, I took a keen interest in it myself and was anxious to make it more popular he began noticeably to thaw and even to give me a certain amount of his confidence.

Despite the unpropitious start to our friendship my own interest in him had been firmly caught on that first afternoon. Superficially he was not attractive, his behaviour had been rather gauche and yet there was something about him that commanded attention. Here, I felt, was personality of an unusual kind. Certainly after this I should not follow Miss Sarah's advice and sacrifice the violin to the 'pyahno'.

The difficulty, however, was to know how enthusiasm could be aroused. The violin lessons were unpopular and the girls who took them a dreary little company who sawed away to the general discomfort in distant rooms. How could a more encouraging atmosphere be created? Suddenly an idea occurred to me. When Captain Cook wished to overcome the reluctance of his crew to drink the lime juice which he knew would cure them of scurvy, he drank it himself and ordered his officers to follow his example. I did not order my staff to learn the violin but I decided to take some further lessons myself. My playing was far from satisfactory at this, or any other time and it seemed possible that I might at once help myself and encourage a warmer interest in the instrument, might possibly serve as a buffer between the master and his somewhat intimidated pupils and might certainly be in a better position to observe.

Miss Sarah left The Mount at the end of the summer term of 1891. There was an absence of speech-making or of presentations which must have saddened so grand and impressive a headmistress. I think most of us felt a certain relief and it was in this mood of new-found freedom that I made my suggestion to Mr Elgar. He not only agreed to it but, having tested me as a violinist, invited me to join the Ladies' Orchestral Class which he was then forming in Worcester and of which I became a foundation member.

3

The Lessons

With the start of the violin lessons came my first opportunity of studying Edward Elgar at close quarters. The impression made on me at the outset was that he was extremely shy but that his shyness masked the kind of intense pride with which an unhappy man attempts to console himself for feelings of frustration and disappointment. I remember that as he entered the long room in which the lessons were given he assumed a simply tremendous dignity and spoke about all sorts of trifles but that when he came to the actual business of teaching he stammered, picked up ornaments, quickly replaced them and appeared almost unequal to the task in hand. He seemed to me to be a man whose emotional reactions were out of all proportion to the stimulating causes. It was thus very difficult to be at ease with him since he was so manifestly ill at ease with himself. At first I supposed that I might be the only person on whom he produced this effect but I soon found that it was fairly general.

My musical position at this time was that of an amateur who, having acquired considerable facility on the pianoforte—I had studied under a pupil of Von Bülow, who had wanted to send me on to Clara Schumann—was now proposing to conquer the violin. The thought of my temerity in supposing that I could gate-crash this entirely different technique in a few lessons appals me today. At this time however I was confident that I had a feeling for the instrument, and that, with the training I had already had, I only needed a little more guidance to achieve mastery. Mr Elgar, now settled in a house at Malvern Link, was the leading violinist of the district and it seemed reasonable to suppose that he would supply the requisite discipline and training.

In this I soon found that I was mistaken. It was apparent indeed that he had a loathing for any kind of drudgery which alone would have been a hindrance to success had he been a good teacher in other respects. For a short time a sort of lip-service was paid to the study of technique but from the first it was evident that Mr Elgar was very bored with having to teach it. We began by working laboriously through Kreutzer, but Kreutzer soon gave way to the pleasanter and much more congenial practice of running through works in which the interest was musical rather than technical. Sometimes he would accompany me on the piano, sometimes we would play duets for two violins, such as those of Dancla. But in a very short time the one thing we were never studying at all was technique.

I realised in later years where his teaching had failed. At the time however, what struck me was that the instruction he gave me was infinitely less helpful than that of old Stern at Brighton. Mr Elgar had little of the gift for inspiring his pupils with enthusiasm which was so amazingly evident in the pianoforte lessons given many years later at The Mount by George Woodhouse. In Mr Woodhouse's time the dragons had almost to tear the girls away from their master. In Mr Elgar's it was not always easy to induce them to go near him.

What was most disheartening was that he never seemed to take much interest in one's progress. If asked how a passage should be fingered, he would tell me or, more probably, would rattle it off himself with a rather bad grace and expect me to divine the means by which the effect had been produced. This, of course, I could rarely do, with the result that I felt stupid and discouraged. At no time did I have the conviction which it is

the function of good teaching to encourage, that we were
following a carefully planned course which must lead to
success. His helplessness was noticed by my mother who used
to serve sometimes as dragon while he was teaching. Not being
responsible to the parents of his pupils for any want of progress, she could expend all her sympathy on him in his un-
congenial task.

'That young man,' she said after a particularly heartbreaking
lesson, 'ought never to be teaching. I'm very sorry for him.'

What he should have been doing she did not specify and I
myself had not yet realized the direction in which his genius
was driving him.

If the lessons were disappointing as lessons, they were of
absorbing interest for the light they gradually began to shed on
the character of the man who gave them. He was one of the
most repressed people it is possible to imagine and at first was
exceptionally uncommunicative. He was enclosed, as it were,
by a haunting fear of innumerable disapprovals and for weeks
would hardly speak at all. But gradually, as he found that I
represented none of these disapprovals, he became a little more
expansive.

It started with books. I have always been an omniverous
reader and he would pick up volumes that had been left in the
music-room and ask about them. From this it was of course an
easy step to questions of taste and here he often surprised me.
For instance I remember that he condemned *Cavalleria Rusticana*,
the Intermezzo from which was at that time beginning to
achieve its boundless popularity, not on musical grounds which
might have been understandable but because the characters of
the opera were persons in low life.

This struck me as a puzzling point of view but, as I was soon
to find, Mr Elgar was a puzzling person. He had at this time,
and indeed never wholly lost, a marked Worcestershire accent
and was not then a young man of any particular distinction, yet
he had a habit of speaking of Malvern in the condescending

manner of a country gentleman condemned to live in a suburb.

Odder still, to me at any rate, was his reaction to a question about plainsong. Visiting Paris during the Easter before I took the school, I had been deeply impressed by the singing at Saint Sulpice and later asked Mr Elgar to tell me something of the history of the ecclesiastical modes. It was at once clear that he knew a good deal about the subject for he gave me a comprehensive account of their use and meaning. I was very interested and was trying to thank him when he suddenly interrupted me by saying with the jerkiness of embarrassment.

'Yes, but if I tell you how I come to know all this you'll probably never speak to me again.'

Wondering what terrible revelation was to follow, I waited.

'You see,' he said anxiously, 'we are Catholics, my wife and I.'

I could hardly help laughing. But also I felt rather shocked at his supposing me capable of such bigotry and I said so.

He replied that I little knew how seriously his career had been hampered by his Catholicism. He told me of post after post which would have been open to him but for the prejudice against his religion, of golden opportunities snatched from his grasp by inferior men of more acceptable views. It was a subject on which he evidently felt very bitter for he embroidered it at great length.

I listened and I wondered. . . . It was the first occasion on which he had spoken to me of himself and, while I was glad that he should do so if it gave him any relief, I could not help feeling that there was a strain of morbidity in what he was saying. It was impossible not to sympathize with him. I did not doubt that he had in fact suffered as a result of his faith. But at the back of my mind was an uneasy feeling that he took a certain pleasure in dramatizing these humiliations.

Then, anxious not to be unfair to him, I resolved to suspend judgement until I knew him better.

This little outburst marked a stage in the development of our friendship. Hitherto he had always kept the conversation on a strictly impersonal plane but now that the ice had been broken he began to speak with ever greater freedom, the stiffness of his voice and manner relaxed and we found ourselves gradually reaching a far more friendly footing. Very soon, indeed, the lessons became little more than talks, first about music and then about ourselves and our aims.

It amuses me to reflect in the light of later knowledge that this was an encounter between two extremely conceited young people, each of whom was desperately anxious to impress the other. I was very young and wished to make it clear that in addition to being the headmistress I knew something about music and that I had had what I fondly supposed to be a wide listening experience. He on the other hand was equally concerned to make me realize that he was no mere provincial but the musical equal of anyone I had heard or met.

It is a tribute to his quality that I was impressed by this despite the fact that I had heard practically every artist of note who was before the public at that time and, in consequence, a considerable proportion of the classical repertory of chamber-music. I could tell him of young Mr Paderewski's astounding playing of Chopin, of Sarasate's silky tone, of the Joachim Quartet and their famous Stradivarii, of the Monday Pops at the St James's Hall, of Mme Norman Neruda, the first of the eminent women violinists and of Sir Charles Hallé's 'clear, cold and classical' playing of the Beethoven sonatas, surrounded by Burne-Jones's troops of spineless damsels in the Grosvenor Gallery.

Like most concert-goers of that time, and incidentally far too many today, I was then much more interested in executants than in the works which served as an excuse for their virtuosity. I was therefore rather surprised to find Mr Elgar completely unimpressed by what I told him. It was clear that he wished me to think that he knew quite as much about the artists of the day as I—a piece of rather pathetic pretension which did not deceive me for a moment—but also that he regarded executants, those gods of the great public, as creatures of an altogether inferior breed. In view of the fact that it was, after all, as a trainer of executants that he had appeared on our scene this came as something of a shock. He was quite firm on the point however.

'The artist, the true artist,' he said, truthfully enough but with a somewhat trying superiority of manner, 'is not the executant but the composer.'

He then went on to tell me, a little haltingly at first, that this was the branch of music in which he felt that his own future lay. He told me of various small successes he had already made, of performances here and there, of a struggle against almost insuperable obstacles raised by his determination to write what he wished rather than what was demanded.

Warming to his theme, he walked up and down the room, sometimes pausing at the windows to look at the high background of hill, then returning and telling me with a curious ferocity of his hopes and ambitions. I felt strangely touched. Although Brahms, Tchaikovsky and Greig were all then still alive, it had somehow never occurred to me that composers were, or could be, living people whom one might meet. I thought of them as Great Figures of the Past, never of the present. It hardly seemed possible that this young man could be one of them.

I was trying to adjust myself to the situation when he suddenly stopped abruptly and closed up like an oyster. Nothing that I could say would induce him to return to the subject. He seemed to feel that he had been betrayed into making an unwilling confidence.

It was soon to be apparent that these bewildering changes of emotional direction in conversation were by no means unusual. Indeed the more I was able to observe him the more I was struck by the conflicting elements in his character. One never quite knew what he would say next or how he would say it.

Sometimes he would be simple and natural, sometimes, when he felt ill at ease, he would become absurdly portentous and forbidding.

One day he asked me with the greatest formality if I would grant him a favour. His manner suggested something very prodigious but I have always been reckless so, without asking what the favour was, I said, 'Yes.'

He paused nervously, stammered and then told me that he would be particularly grateful if I would give him a bunch of the syringa which grew in the drive. . . . So simple a request in the wake of so much preparation made me smile but I gravely said I should be delighted. While I was cutting it and adding a few other flowers he explained that he wanted to take something to his wife which would remind her of the gardens and parks to which she was accustomed. It appeared that she felt unconscionably cramped in the small houses to which they had been condemned since their marriage. Again I wondered. . . .

The incident, though trivial, was typical of his habit of taking everything *au grand sérieux*. I often felt that had he been able to cultivate a lighter touch in his daily round he would have been spared much of the unhappiness which clouded his life.

One day, however, he showed me a simpler and altogether more attractive facet of his character, though even here there was a chilling aftermath. A sale of work in aid of some charity or other was being prepared at the school and one of my own contributions was a quilt for a child's cot. It was embroidered in squares each of which illustrated a fairy-tale.

Mr Elgar chanced to see the quilt, which, as it happened, was already sold, and was very interested in it.

'I should like to buy that for my little girl,' he said.

I told him that I didn't know he had a little girl.

'Oh yes,' he said rather naïvely, 'she is the most beautiful baby there ever was.'

Later when I saw the child being taken out in her perambulator I felt that for once the parent's proverbially blind eye had not misled him. She was in fact a very beautiful little girl with flaxen hair and a roseleaf complexion, but the expression on her face troubled me for it was one of profound sadness. She never smiled or laughed and, when I learned that from the first she had been taught never to make the least noise for fear of disturbing her father, I understood her unnatural look of resignation.

With an insensibility to the value of English words which he never overcame, Mr Elgar formed a habit of torturing them into anagrammatic patterns, but the name he found for his daughter was one of his happier efforts in this direction. In 1889 he had made a portmanteau-word of the first and last syllables of his wife's Christian names (Caroline Alice) and used it for the dedication of *Salut D'Amour*. When later their daughter was born he remembered the charming word and she was christened Carice!

The duality which allowed him at once to take a pride in his daughter and to be unable to bear the sound of her voice was wholly typical.

If the violin lessons had given me some insight into Elgar's character as a man, it was at the Ladies' Orchestral Class that I first realized his quality as a composer. I used to share a desk at these meetings with a girl whom we may call Jessie Mouseley and as the Mouseleys were typical of one section of the society which surrounded Elgar at this time a sketch of them may not be wholly out of place.

They lived in a semi-detached house, with a monkey-puzzle tree in the front garden, overlooking Malvern Link Common, were smugly respectable and almost completely wanting in imagination. Some desire for expression, however, must have been felt by the younger members of the family and this they satisfied with music. Musically, indeed, they were in everything in the district. They sang, they played, and when, later on, musical festivals were introduced, they not only entered every class but held indignation meetings outside the hall afterwards because no Mouseley had won a prize or even favourable mention. Albert Mouseley subsequently went on the stage and I remember seeing him at the Haymarket Theatre. His sisters said that although he only played the part of a footman you could see that he was really a gentleman.

One afternoon at the orchestral class Jessie and I found ourselves playing in a work which was unfamiliar at any rate to me. I think I must have arrived late and commenced hurriedly for I do not remember looking at the title but I do remember the profound impression its rather Mendelssohnian slow movement made on me.

'What is this?' I asked.

'Oh, it's a thing he wrote himself,' she said. *'Serenade for Strings.'*

She spoke casually and quite without enthusiasm.

'Wrote it himself?' I could scarcely believe it.

'Oh yes. He's always writing these things and trying them out on us.'

She seemed to take it so much as a matter of course that I almost wondered if my own judgement had been at fault. But as we drove back to Malvern and the theme of that *larghetto* sang through my mind I remembered what Mr Elgar had said about his ambitions and I became very thoughtful indeed.

By the end of 1892 I had come to know Mr Elgar exceedingly well but there was no gainsaying the fact that he was one of the most difficult problems that faced me in the management of the school. The *Serenade for Strings* had convinced me that he had an exceptional talent with which it might be an inspiration to be associated but it was evident that he was prevented from exerting any influence for good by his hatred of teaching. I believe he said in later life that to him teaching had been what turning a grindstone might be to a man with a dislocated shoulder. The simile was intended, no doubt, to provoke sympathy. It does not seem to have occurred to him that such a grinder might injure the tools given him to sharpen, yet it was with these, of course, that I was concerned.

It was clear, then, that if he were to provide the inspiration we must supply the enthusiasm. Taking lessons myself had been the first small step but something more was needed and it was at this point that I hit on the idea of a school orchestra. I was in some doubt as to how he would react to the suggestion for he was, as I have said, extremely difficult and uncertain. To my surprise he welcomed it.

4

Ensemble

The school ensemble class was immense fun. The sharp line which separates chamber music from orchestral music was completely disregarded, our activities being governed mainly by the number of players who happened to be available. Thus, if there were only the nuclear four, we would grind through a Haydn or a Mozart quartet or Mr Elgar himself might play the piano part with us in the Schumann Quintet. Later, as our numbers increased, we began to study such works as Schubert's Fifth Symphony, then a good deal less popular than it has since become, or even Mozart's Symphony in G. Minor.

The class, 'Little Orchy' as it came to be called, was limited to girls at The Mount but it served as the basis of a larger body known as 'Big Orchy' which was open to those outside and which ultimately became much in demand for concerts, bazaars and amateur dramatic performances in the surrounding district. With this, however, Mr Elgar had nothing to do. Among those who regularly played in Big Orchy were my dear friend Isabel Fitton (later to become the Ysobel of the Enigma Variations) and her sister Hilda. Visitors who joined us included George Alder, the horn-player, who was destined to arrange the first meeting between Elgar and Arnold Bax.

We soon found that Mr Elgar was far happier with the ensemble class than he had ever been with individual pupils. For one thing the personal relation was easier with a class which could be cursed roundly as a body without its bursting into tears, and there was another even more important. As a teacher he was merely the suffering and helpless witness of the struggles of his pupils whereas in the ensemble class he himself became an active participant. In our early days when we could muster only a few weak and dubious strings it was necessary to have a sort of continuo to hold us together and this Mr Elgar provided at the piano in a particularly attractive way. Later when with increasing numbers and competency we attempted fuller scores, he filled in the missing parts and did so with immense skill, but in the meantime he had to be content with supporting our stumbling efforts and decorating the simple works we played with impromptu counterpoints and figurations. It may be noted, however regretfully, that he was not above adding these to a Haydn quartet and that, despite his lifelong contempt for the piano and for those composers whose orchestral writing showed a keyboard influence, it was nearly always the piano rather than the violin that he chose to play at our meetings.

He loved doing this and often became so absorbed in the intricacies of his invention that he seemed to forget our presence. Sometimes when one of us produced a particularly painful squawk he would look round with a petrifying scowl and say, 'What do you think you are doing?' And sometimes, when things had gone unusually well, he might even smile.

The question of how Edward Elgar acquired his mastery of orchestration has never, perhaps, been quite satisfactorily answered and I am certainly not going to claim that the practice with our school orchestra had anything to do with it. That mastery is already apparent in the *Froissart* overture which had been written in 1890. Elgar himself told me that he had acquired the greater part of his knowledge of the subject as the result of that extraordinary appointment of 1879 to the bandmastership of the Worcester Lunatic Asylum. The band at the asylum was composed not of the patients but of the officials; its constitution, however, could hardly have been crazier had it been

planned by the inmates. According to Mr W. H. Reed it consisted of first and second violins (without the support of violas
or 'cellos), flute, oboe and clarinet, first and second cornets,
euphonium, bombardon, double bass and piano. And this was
before the time of Stravinsky!

This horrific collection of disparate sonorities (in which Mr
Basil Maine sees the origin of the scarecrow army in *Falstaff*)
had somehow to be combined into an acceptable ensemble, a
medium for applying the therapeutic effect of music to the
patients. The young conductor had himself to score the pieces
performed and, although it must have been a tiresome task, it
taught him one of the most valuable lessons of his life. In adapt-
ing normal orchestral scores to the limitations of his singular
band in such a way as to make the result sound bearable he had
to know to a hair's breadth what each of the instruments could
do both in solo and in concert. The study of those instruments
and the intimate knowledge of unusual tonal combinations thus
acquired laid the foundation of that mastery of orchestration
which is noticeable in even his earliest works.

The ensemble class at The Mount could help him with no
problems of this kind—other than the problem of bad string
playing. One thing that we were able to do for him, however,
was probably helpful. This was that we were always willing
to provide him with whatever score he might wish at the
moment to study. Again and again works which were wildly
beyond the scope of our players would be hired from Goodwin
and Tabb's for purposes which were not at first clear to us.
We set our teeth and grimly played the notes—or as many of
them as we could manage—but Mr Elgar was too happy at the
piano with the full score open before him to be troubled by us.
With that exceptional faculty of inner hearing, to which Ernest
Newman has drawn attention, he was examining the means by
which every orchestral effect had been produced and was stor-
ing the knowledge for future use.

Sometimes it would be hard to understand what dictated his

choice. I remember, for instance, that on one occasion he was anxious to see of all things, the overture to Gounod's *Mireille*. What he wanted this for I do not know and cannot imagine. More complex scores would be eagerly scanned on arrival and exhaustively analysed.

It has more than once been said that Elgar never showed any sign of the personal eccentricity which is usually noticeable in artists. So far is this from being true that by 1892, six years before he wrote the Enigma Variations, we had already nick-named him the Genius. It was because he was so manifestly a genius, indeed, that we put up with eccentricities that would have been tolerated in none of the other visiting masters. Mr Basil Maine is nearer the mark in saying that he was not a bohemian and of this I can give two examples. In the first place, although he was in the orchestra of the Three Choirs Festival, he always tried to avoid carrying a violin case about with him for fear of looking like a musician. In the second place he re-fused to wear the kind of sober dark clothes adopted by the other visiting masters and usually dressed as nearly as possible in the style of a country gentleman. On one occasion indeed he caused considerable excitement at the school by arriving in a golfing suit—the breeches and long gaiters which were worn prior to the introduction of plus-fours. The news got round quickly and by the time he left a good many girls had found vantage points overlooking the drive. There was much discus-sion as to whether using a violin bow was any training for a golf-club and in general I think the incident made his pupils feel that he was rather more human than they had supposed.

But it is absurd to pretend that he was not 'temperamental'. The canary which annoyed him had to be rushed out of the room, draughts had to be rigidly excluded and, as soon as the class was over, tea served without a moment's delay. Even with the utmost care for his whims one could not always ensure a smooth practice. On one occasion he was so annoyed by the quality of the playing that he jumped up and walked out of the house. I got the girls together after this and rehearsed them thoroughly to avoid the repetition of such an incident. The next time he came the music went with a flourish and he was amiability itself. But I am quite certain that it never occurred to him for one instant that the faulty playing had been in any way a reflection on his teaching.

Very occasionally, when a subject really interested him, he would become animated and really helpful. At these times light broke through the clouds indeed and shone upon the poor little class.

'Now then, second violins and violas,' he would say, 'this crescendo passage depends on you. Don't forget that the higher strings are already doing their utmost and that it is you who must swell the body of sound.'

The class was delighted with hints of this kind and would have welcomed more. Unfortunately they were all too rarely offered.

He never at any time had much of that sense of humour which eases difficult moments in class but, when he was happy, would sometimes be boisterous or facetious. Thus when some of the girls who had not learned to carry their fiddles under the arm came into the room holding them awkwardly by the neck, he said, 'I do wish you wouldn't hold those things as if they were legs of mutton.'

Then again he would relapse into his shy and rather morose habit. I have never known anyone, indeed, who changed so abruptly and completely. In some degree these changes may have been due to nervousness for he had to exert great control, I believe, in order not to stammer when he was excited, with the result that he would often speak in a stilted, rather measured style. In the main, however, they were due to fluctuations of mood. And the prevailing mood appeared to be one of acute unhappiness.

I was a good deal concerned over this unhappiness but felt powerless to help him. The only thing one could do was to

remove every cause of annoyance from his immediate surroundings and hope for the best. Even then he would often show
irritation over matters so trifling that one could hardly believe
them to be its true cause. It seemed evident that he was suffering
from some overwhelming secret trouble but what this was I
had no means of knowing and he was so cold and aloof as to
make it seem improbable that I ever should.

Then one day after the ensemble practice he lingered on over
tea, silent and diffident. I did not try to make conversation as I
felt fairly certain that nothing I could say would find favour. . . .
Suddenly, without knowing quite how it had begun, I found
myself listening to an outpouring of misery that was positively
heartrending. Gone were the usual reserve, the hauteur and
superiority. In their place was a raw and almost frightening
sincerity.

It was a story, none the less vivid for being disjointed and
incoherent, of frustrated ambition. The one thing he wanted to
do in life, the be-all and end-all of his existence, was to write
great music. For this he had lived, worked and suffered, had
abandoned the shelter of safe employment, had risked the dis-
pleasure of his parents and had plunged headlong into a difficult
and uncertain way of life. The creation of music had become a
veritable passion with him. He felt himself swayed by an urge
which, if obeyed, must carry him to a goal undreamt of by the
journeymen-composers of his time.

And yet, in spite of this urge, in spite of the glorious possibilities which he knew to be almost within his reach, he had
come to a standstill and could do nothing. Flounderingly, for
he was in a pitifully overwrought state, he told me of his struggle
to achieve a musical career. It had always seemed hopeless.
Starting with an ambition to become a concert-violinist he had
taken lessons in Worcester but had felt them to be inadequate
and had scraped and saved in order that he might study in
London under Pollitzer, a distinguished Hungarian professor
of that time. His little store of money gave out before the new

master had been able to do much more than upset his own style of playing and destroy his confidence, and he returned to Worcester, utterly discouraged, to pick up what living was possible in the hated role of teacher and occasional performer.

Ultimately he began to realize that he was not a potential concert-violinist, not even a teacher, but a composer and nothing else. The realization brought no satisfaction for he knew that, little as he could make by teaching music, he would earn far less by writing it and the drudgery of teaching prevented his being able to compose. Without money and the leisure that money provides indeed, he believed that he would never be able to do so.

'And then,' he said as if it were the climax of his misfortunes, 'I married.'

It was quite impossible to make any reply to this so I did not attempt one.

It appeared that his wife had an income of her own which she was only too willing to dedicate to the cause of freeing him for his true vocation. Selling his teaching connection in Worcester and Malvern therefore, he had gone with her to London in the hope of at last establishing himself. The aim of becoming a concert-violinist was as yet by no means completely displaced and it was planned that he should take a few engagements to help out their means until he could make a living by composition.

The plan was doomed to disaster. The income which had been sufficent for one proved inadequate for two, and his wife's inexperience as a housekeeper had been a further handicap. He told me of his wearisomely unsuccessful journeys in search of engagements, of the further complication of their difficulties by the birth of a child, above all of the crushing discovery that, even had he been able to sell his compositions, the anxieties of the home had completely deprived him of his power to produce them. Finally, hearing from his friend, D'Egville that the teaching connection in Worcester and Malvern had been abandoned

by his absconding successor and was therefore to be had for
the taking, he had thrown in his hand and had returned once
more to the hated routine, completely defeated.

'Now it's all finished—utterly finished,' he concluded dis-
consolately.

I could not help feeling deeply moved by such a cry of despair,
indeed over fifty years later the memory of it is still painfully
vivid, but I felt that some kind of attempt had to be made to
comfort him and to pull him out of his slough of despond.

'Oh no,' I said, 'it isn't finished. It's only beginning.'

It was not particularly easy to talk to him because his conviction of failure was so intense that he was in no mood to listen
to encouragement. But by this time I was determined to rouse
him from his misery and apathy. The means I used were not
very subtle but I was deeply troubled and spoke with determination and sincerity. I said that I was convinced he was
destined for greatness and that he must rise and be worthy of
it. I pointed out that genius had always had to overcome great
difficulties and that, if he thought even for a moment of what
composers like Mozart and Schubert had suffered in the way of
poverty, neglect and misunderstanding, his own afflictions
would seem less unbearable. I did not minimize those afflictions
but I tried to make him feel that they need not be quite the
brake on his work that they seemed. If only he would try to
forget his conviction of failure and would take a lighter view of
his problems and difficulties he would find his lost powers
returning.

It has to be admitted that what I offered was rather cold
comfort but it made its effect. Pressing my hand, a little dramati-
cally, he said that I had helped him more than I knew and that
now he would go and work. . . .

It is a wholly typical irony that, during this period which he had
described as completely barren, he had actually written *Froissart,
My Love Dwelt in a Northern Land*, the *Serenade for Strings*, and

many of the other early works by which he is now known. But, although I guessed that he was exaggerating, I also felt that there was a basis of essential truth in what he was saying and I began to feel a sympathy for him which he subsequently never wholly lost.

5

Background

In attempting to give a faithful picture of Edward Elgar as he appeared to those who knew him intimately one is confronted sooner or later with a problem to which there is no very easy solution. His earliest biographer, R. J. Buckley, noticed that there were many Dr Elgars, and Mr Frank Howes has pointed out in an excellent critical analysis that two of them wrote music. Of the characteristics that made up the complete man, many were extremely lovable, the boyish facetiousness that comes out in many of the early letters, the healthy love of the Malvern countryside, and indeed of wholesome things in general, the wistfulness that is often the keynote of his music, and much else. But there was another side to his nature which, superficially at any rate, was far less attractive, and it is this which constitutes the problem.

If the portrait is to seem at all kindly one has to choose between trying to omit all reference to the less attractive features or else including them frankly while trying to explain as sympathetically as possible the causes from which they sprang. The first course—which has been followed by nearly all the biographers, other than those like Gerald Cumberland who have indulged in wholesale denigration—has the disadvantage of first misleading the reader and then of baffling him when some unavoidable flaw slips into prominence. Thus W. H. Reed's excellent *Elgar*, written by a loyal and devoted friend, introduces us to a character so lovable that we are at a complete loss to understand that character's ill-bred behaviour at a civic function in Worcester and at a dog-show. And even Mrs Richard Powell, whose valuable little book, though far less fully documented than Reed's, is written much more objectively, does nothing to prepare us for the shock of reading that Elgar deliberately and callously hurt her hand out of sheer spite at Hereford.

The second course—of trying to include all the contradictory features—requires a profound understanding of Elgar's extremely complex character and is therefore far more difficult to follow but, since it is the only one that can yield anything like a complete picture it has been unhesitatingly though somewhat anxiously, chosen by the writers of the present study.

A curious point about Elgar's biographers is that few of them, whether over-lenient or over-censorious, seem to realize the precise relation to his character of its less attractive side. Thus Gerald Cumberland, whose *Set Down in Malice* contains a savage attack on Elgar's snobbery which is by no means entirely unjustified, writes as if snobbery were the beginning and end of his character. And W. H. Reed, who can hardly admit any faults at all in his hero, persistently sees them as lovable little surface blemishes of no real importance. It seems to have occurred to no one that they should be regarded as a part of the complete man and a measure of the intense suffering which ran through the whole of his life.

To present him as a benevolent old country gentleman with charming manners who somehow found time to turn out a large quantity of music is to take seriously the mask which he himself ultimately adopted in order to conceal the misery which lay behind. So far from being anything of the kind, he was in reality a musical fanatic whose energy was constantly frustrated by the frightful respectability of the provincial milieu into which he happened to be projected and whose music was often, as it were, torn out of the misery caused by this conflict.

I did not discover the source of this misery till many years after the scenes which have so far been described—until round about 1900 in fact when the accident of our both buying bicycles led to a joint exploration of the Malvern country which threw us together for days on end—but since the influences which formed his attitude to life have an important bearing on what follows, it has been thought well to try and analyse them before proceeding further.

Edward Elgar was born at Broadheath only twenty years after Queen Victoria's accession to the throne. The cottage, arranged as an Elgar museum, looks attractive today, but in 1857 it was the home of a small tradesman who had a music shop in Worcester three miles away. Dr Colles in *Grove's Dictionary* describes old Mr Elgar as 'a musician of the type in which fortunately this country is rich, who, without seeking or attaining any personal eminence, do sterling work in the provincial centres. He founded a successful music-selling business in Worcester, was organist of St George's Roman Catholic Church there, and also a capable violinist.' Except that the successful music-selling business was a tiny shop which was never far above the water-line of solvency, this is true enough as seen from the viewpoint of our own age. But it is not by any means how the matter would have looked to superior persons of those times in Worcester, and it was unfortunately these who were to provide a painful environment for Mr Elgar's fifth child.

Today, when social distinctions seem to be fading from existence, it is hard to understand the rigidity with which they were maintained during the reign of Queen Victoria. A glance at the pages of *Punch*, however, will show among other things that, in those years, to be born in a wrong social stratum was an almost unforgivable offence, a sin for which there was no expiation. And if ever there was a wrong social stratum, it was that inhabited by a provincial tradesman, and in this case one whose business paid so badly that his whole family had ultimately to be concentrated into the few small rooms over the shop. The situation was further aggravated by the fact that the Elgars were Catholics in a Protestant community and thus almost as completely isolated from those who might have been considered their social equals as they were from the aristocratic and exclusive families of the Malvern district.

The point is of enormous importance to any understanding of Edward Elgar because of its effect on his subsequent outlook upon life. Whatever talent he might possess, whatever his dreams and hopes, he felt himself branded as something very like a social pariah. It is easy for us, living long after the event, to see that his reaction to this handicap was mistaken and indeed disastrous, but we must remember that he had an artist's heightened sensibility. His work as a musician inevitably brought him into contact with people who were as much his superiors socially as they were his inferiors aesthetically, and their easy manners and scarcely veiled contempt caused him a misery and resentment from which he never wholly shook himself free.

Had he been a more courageous and stolid, less sensitive type of youth, he might have disregarded his handicap and gone steadily forward with his life's interests—but then such a youth could not have written his music. With Edward the reaction was different and seems to have been very complex. In the first place his sensibility had evidently been so badly hurt that to the end of his life he shrouded it in many layers of hard outer pretence—the pretence that many of his friends seem to have taken for the real man, but which in fact made him nearly impossible to know at all intimately. But inside this shell, and occasionally bursting through it in a distorted form, were terrible bitternesses against his father for being a tradesman and against those who had had better advantages than he. In later life these bitternesses took the form of a belief noticed by many of his friends that there were actually malignant forces working against him and gave rise to a number of convictions about life which were injurious to his work and happiness. Because the home had been poor and undistinguished he came to attach an undue value to everything in which it was deficient—money, social position and their manifestations in sport, club-life and a host of other diversions which were foreign to his true nature. And in painful conflict with these feelings was a strong filial devotion to his parents.

His biographers have described the remarkable tenacity with which, knowing no academy other than his father's shop, the young man trained himself by the exercise of severe self-discipline into mastery of the technical details of his art. That this discipline had not been relaxed even when he was thirty-five I can testify, since it was I who lent him some of the books (for example Cherubini's *Counterpoint and Fugue*) that Mr Basil Maine quotes as having influenced him. But what seems to me even more remarkable is that this persistent self-improvement should have been exercised despite the dulling effect of the feelings of inferiority and discouragement arising from the unhelpful background provided by his home.

It is impossible by now to reconstruct the atmosphere of that home, partly because, in common with most of the friends whom he met after he had married and settled elsewhere, I was never asked into it, and partly because one may suspect that he himself, finding that he did not care to think of it exactly as it was, tended to take refuge in delusions of grandeur, clothing it with a culture that it can hardly have possessed. Of his mother, a farmer's daughter from Herefordshire, he always spoke with respect and affection. He never took me to see her but I was with him in Worcester when he paid one of his last calls on her before she died and I am certain that he loved her deeply. There is a tradition that she was well-read and it seems certain that it was she who introduced what comfort there was into the home.

One gathers that there was not a great deal and this was unfortunate as the Elgars, cut off by their faith from the life which revolved about the Cathedral and crowded together, were thrown largely on their own resources. Old Mr Elgar, for

all the beauty of his face in the early portrait on view at Broadheath, seems to have been a very irascible man. I never met
him, but Mr D'Egville, the dancing master at The Mount, who
had played in a small string band that Mr Elgar senior conducted, gave me a little vignette of the old man that I have
always remembered. He said that at one of the rehearsals, having put up less and less patiently with some bad playing, Mr
Elgar finally danced with rage and exclaimed, 'Oh why don't
you cut your nails?'

For Edward, dreaming of a larger and more beautiful life, I
think the rooms over the shop at No. 10 High Street can never
have held much happiness. Music-making was the escape which
the young Elgars found from the dreariness of their life and I
have often felt that there was something profoundly touching
in their efforts to find in music a beauty which was lacking in
their surroundings. That they did in fact find it there is no doubt
for they formed their own ensemble, having learnt to play
various instruments and, lacking a double bass, even made one
out of packing cases. This exploration without academic guidance of new musical worlds was a splendid achievement, but to
Edward it had one serious disadvantage.

The self-made man is usually impatient—and often unjustly
so—of rivals who have been helped to an equal success. Now
if ever there was a self-made musician it was Edward, who
hardly had any lessons except on the violin throughout the
whole of his formative years. Had he been able to attend one of
the great music schools, he might have learnt nothing about
music that he did not teach himself at home but, in contact with
other musicians, he might have had many corners rubbed off,
might have learned a greater tolerance and might have been
more willing to believe that those who criticized his work were
not necessarily part of the malignant force that appeared to be
working against him. Unfortunately these advantages were
denied him and the want of them caused him acute suffering
through out his life.

Such, then, were some of the influences that moulded the young Elgar and it is difficult to see how with his particular equipment he could have reacted to them in any other way. A further influence of great importance was to come into his life but that belongs to a later chapter.

6

Early Successes

If Edward Elgar often tended to exaggerate the difficulties that delayed his success as a composer, those difficulties were none the less real. The years from 1890 (when *Froissart* was produced at the Three Choirs Festival in Worcester but killed by the small dimensions of the Shire Hall) to 1896 (when the first decisive hit outside the Malvern neighbourhood was made with *King Olaf* at Hanley) were studded with a number of small local successes which, however, never seemed to build up into a connected series, still less to carry his fame outside the provincial circle in which he moved. The earliest of these successes that came within my own experience was a performance of the *Spanish Serenade* which was given at Hereford.

My presence was the result of a tiff typical of many in the early years of our friendship. The Genius was, as I have said, a man self-made in spite of many handicaps. It was thus really hard for him to see the viewpoint of others or either to avoid hurting their feelings or apologize when he had done so, and there were in consequence times when relations between us became strained. I soon found that the most effective way of dealing with his more difficult moods was to ignore him as far as possible, since at heart he was bitterly lonely and could not bear for long to forgo the sympathy and understanding he needed. Even so he would never refer in any way to the disagreement but would make some touching little overture of friendship which one could not very well resist.

I forget the cause of the quarrel on this occasion but the peace-offering was an octavo roll of music which he almost furtively put into my hand.

'I don't know if this will interest you,' he said.

Unrolling the paper I found a copy, fresh from the printers, of his *Spanish Serenade*. My name had been written at the top right-hand corner.

He explained that the Herefordshire Philharmonic Society were to sing the work in a few days and that if I cared to go over to Hereford to hear it he could give me a ticket for the concert and an invitation to tea afterwards with some friends. I was naturally delighted with such an offer—and perhaps too with the reconcilation, for I liked him—and accepted it on the spot.

Hereford is the most remote of the Three Choirs cities and in many ways the most charming, not having been industralized like Worcester and Gloucester. I had never been there before and was glad of an excuse for going. The cathedral, I found, was inferior to the other two but the town with its medieval streets and its charming old houses made me think of a water-colour by David Cox. The County-cum-cathedral-close atmosphere gave me a foretaste of the circumstances in which many of Elgar's early works were to be produced.

He himself had gone over earlier in the day for the rehearsal, the Hereford orchestra being at that time one of those which he led, and I made my way to the hall alone. There was a com-fortably large and well-dressed audience, the members of which all seemed to know each other and the atmosphere was easy and pleasant. I sat in front of two ladies, who, evidently not having met for some time, were inclined to regard the music as an interruption to their conversation.

I cannot say that the *Spanish Serenade* impressed me as the *Serenade for Strings* had done but I thought it a pleasingly original piece of music. The words, although by Longfellow, a poet from whose work Elgar was to draw some of his most disastrous libretti, were more felicitous than usual and the setting, so different with its suggestion of guitars and southern warmth from the ordinary choral music of the time, seemed to me curiously authentic. Many years later when I lived in Portugal and heard serenades actually played in the streets I realized how faithfully Elgar, who had never been near the Iberian Peninsula, had caught the evening atmosphere of its towns. I have forgotten everything else that was sung that afternoon. The *Spanish Serenade* remains a vivid and haunting memory.

The two ladies behind me seemed less interested in the music than in its composer. What appeared to strike them as remarkable, however, was, not that he could write music, but that he had married a member of their own social circle. This caught my attention. In the early days of the school I had been too much concerned with my own personal problems there to find time for social contacts and it had not occurred to me at first that the Genius might be married. When later he began to speak of his wife and to imply a distinguished social background it was evident that he had a great admiration for her. He told me that she was a good linguist, that she was interested in literature and that he wanted us to meet as he felt we should appreciate each other. But strange as it may seem, the meeting had still not taken place at the time of this concert and the lady whom my two neighbours were discussing so freely was not personally known to me.

In those days women of the upper classes had not formed the habit of eloping with dance-band leaders, chauffeurs and prize-fighters, and it was evident that the two ladies behind me felt that in marrying a mere musician their friend had committed what must be considered at least an error of taste. This seemed to me extremely hard on the poor Genius, and I listened fascinated, wondering whether further revelations would follow.

They did, quantities of them. It seemed that Mrs Elgar was the daughter of dear old Lady Roberts of Redmarley who would

certainly not have allowed such a marriage had she been alive
to prevent it. Friends of the family had simply not known what
to do. They did not wish to cut Alice Roberts—though apparently a good many of them had done so—but they naturally
felt that they could not be expected to meet a man whose father
kept a wretched little shop in Worcester and even tuned their
pianos. It was all *most* awkward.

When the concert was finished I left the hall turning this
conversation over in my mind. So this was the set into which
the Genius had married. I wondered what effect it would have—
was already having—on his development as an artist. These
people had an ease and finish which made him look rather
gauche. But a genius I nevertheless believed him to be and I
could not help seeing that if these were his wife's friends they
might prove a serious danger to him unless she herself were
strong-minded enough to cut adrift from their standards and
adopt those of an artist's wife. If she did not he would be torn
between the desire on the one hand to follow his own bent
and on the other to attempt to identify himself with a class to
which he did not belong and which, having no real appreciation
of the value of his genius, might by their sheer assumption of
superiority make him ashamed of it.

These thoughts took additional colour from the tea-party
which followed in a very beautiful eighteenth-century house
near the cathedral. It was the sort of tea-party which is found
only in England and even here only in a few centres. The house,
the furniture, the silver and the china all had the grace of things
which are old and of which great care has always been taken.
The conversation was polite and animated. Lady Mary would
be back next week—the Dean was having trouble again with
those tiresome lay vicars—such a frightful thing about poor
Colonel Francis—the new people at The Spinney were delightful—the Bishop had absolutely condemned it . . . and so on.
I do not remember that there was a passing reference to music,
even the music that had been heard that afternoon. The Genius

brought me a cup of tea but spent most of the time in a corner talking to a man I did not know.

After this I was naturally anxious to see for myself the brave woman who had defied her friends and married the man she loved, but although she was pointed out to me by Jessie Mouseley at the first performance of *The Black Knight* in Worcester, I was not to meet her for some months. All I saw in the distance was a short fair woman in a rose-coloured velvet dress.

The Black Knight, like the *Spanish Serenade*, was a setting of verses by Longfellow but, whereas the libretto of the earlier work had some claim to be called poetry, that of the latter, as anyone may see who looks it up, could hardly be considered anything but doggerel. Surprisingly enough, however, the deficiencies of this translation of Uhland did not turn out to be a handicap. Despite the array of authorities, whom Elgar was to quote later on in support of *Falstaff*, he was strangely wanting in any understanding of poetry and indeed of any sense of verbal rhythms. Again and again when setting verses of quality he would break up their natural rhythm and re-mould it to the curve of his own melody. Thus a jogging measure like that of *The Black Knight* having no particular colour of its own, could the better be illuminated by the splendour of his music.

The work had been taken up by Dr Blair (to whom it was dedicated), the organist of Worcester Cathedral and the Worcester Festival Choral Society which he conducted, and its performance in the Shire Hall was an altogether more important occasion than that of the *Spanish Serenade* at Hereford. Elgar described his cantata as a symphony for chorus and orchestra and it was certainly symphonic in character, an indication of the direction in which his wishes really lay. Mr Dunhill has regretted that Elgar did not recast *The Black Knight* in a purely instrumental form before he outgrew its idiom and one must admit that had he done so we should have had one more orchestral work of value besides being spared too much repetition of some of Longfellow's silliest words.

The warm reception of that first performance may have been due in part to the fact that the Genius was a Worcester man, for its idiom was altogether too novel to be pleasing to conservative music lovers, many of whom undoubtedly felt that he was going out of his way to make strange sounds. But to the even moderately discerning *The Black Knight*, with its youthful freshness, its striking choral effects and the wealth and colour of its orchestration showed an unmistakable advance on his earlier work.

7

Alice

It was the planning of a holiday that ultimately led to my long-delayed meeting with Mrs Elgar. A few weeks after the first performance of *The Black Knight* I read in some monthly magazine an article on Munich. I had long wanted to see this city with its neighbouring Starnberger See and Bavarian Alps but the article mentioned an additional attraction, for it appeared that during the summer there was to be a Musikfest at which most of Wagner's operas would be given, including even *The Ring*. In those days Munich was not so much visited as it has since become and the addition of music to the charm of a holiday off the beaten track decided me. As moreover, it happened that the parents of a very charming pupil named Alice Davey wanted her to see something of Germany I was assured of a companion for the journey.

On casually mentioning my plans to the Genius one day I found that quite independently of me, he and his wife had been arranging a similar expedition. His interest in Munich centred of course wholly on the Musikfest and, supposing that mine did too, he asked me what I knew of Wagnerian opera. Virtually nothing, I told him and added that this was why I wanted to hear it. When I went on to say that my only experience of Wagner so far had been the first English performance (under Richter) of the *Siegfried Idyll*, to which I had been taken by a cousin, the Genius surprised me by saying that he also had been

present on that occasion. We then found that outside circumstances had made it memorable for both of us. The Genius, who
had been very hard up at the time, had been unable to stay for
the night in London and had come back to Worcester on the
fish and milk train which left Paddington at midnight, while I
had been involved in a rather acrimonious disagreement with
my cousin, a hidebound Handelian who thought the *Idyll* perverse and almost wicked and strongly resented my admiration
for it.

The Genius evidently felt that I had the root of the matter in
me for he plunged at once into an exciting lecture on the theories
behind the new music-drama, its divergence from the older
Italian opera, its use of leading themes—which he illustrated on
the piano with the 'gaze' motive from *Tristan*—and the welding
which was attempted of musical, plastic and dramatic elements
into one art-form. His enthusiasm for the subject, so different
from the dejection he usually exhibited at the school, showed
him in a new and attractive light, which was at once a stimulus
and a challenge to one's power of understanding.

I asked him where he proposed to stay at Munich. He
answered that over this he was in some difficulty. The only
possible place, he felt, was the Vierjahreszeiten, but it would
be altogether too expensive and in any case almost certainly
full. So I told him that my own plan was to go into rooms, of
which I had a number of addresses, supplied by my German
governess, and that, if he chose to do so, he could make use of
my list. He thanked me and suggested that his wife, who had a
good knowledge of German, should call on me. Thus it was
that I first met her.

To describe Alice Elgar in cold blood as she appeared to me
on her first call at The Mount would be to do her a great injustice, for she belonged to a type which has almost completely
disappeared and is now as much an object of derision as the
educational ideals of the school for the daughters of gentlemen
—which she showed every sign of having attended. In order to

understand her at all sympathetically, therefore, one must remember again the rigidity, with which social distinctions were maintained in the reign of Queen Victoria.

Caroline Alice Roberts was the daughter of an Indian Army officer, General Sir Henry Gee Roberts, K.C.B., who after a distinguished career had retired and settled at Hazeldine House, Redmarley, some miles south of the Malvern Hills. General Roberts did not live long to enjoy his retirement and Lady Roberts had also died before Alice met Edward Elgar. (The speculation of one biographer as to whether Alice's parents shared her belief in the young man is thus disposed of.) She was left with a small income and exactly the sort of convictions regarding the paramount importance of caste that one would expect from her training—convictions which were perhaps strengthened by the fact that the very smallness of her income jeopardized her own social position. No one can blame her for observing a scale of values which, however absurd they may seem to us, had been imbibed from her earliest childhood, but perhaps there was a certain irony in her marrying, of all men, Edward Elgar. For the rigidity of the social taboos which were a terrible handicap to her husband, struggling to reach up from the lower rungs of the ladder, had been an even greater handicap to his wife who, trained from the first to regard those less fortunately born than herself as more or less untouchable, never to the end of her life understood the point of view of any social class lower than her own. The attempt to harmonize the two backgrounds was to have a profound effect not only on Elgar's character but on his development as an artist.

Of these facts, however, which in retrospect make Alice Elgar seem a more sympathetic character than she then appeared to me, I knew nothing and my first reaction to her was one of surprise, a surprise, it may be said, which it took me many years to overcome. From what the Genius had told me, from what I had heard at Hereford and elsewhere I had insensibly built up a picture of her as I supposed her to be, but the lady who called at The Mount in the July of 1893 was about as unlike my picture as can be imagined. I had yet to learn, of course, that in descriptions of people the points which are omitted are the most important part of the portrait, and no one had told me what, at first sight, was the most striking thing about Alice Elgar, namely that she was considerably older than her husband. Indeed, as at that time he was an unusually youthful thirty-six and she a rather mature forty-three, she seemed almost to belong to a different generation.

The second factor in my surprise arose from her excessive concern with the etiquette of the situation. Having complimented me on the size of the rooms ('So delightful to see large rooms again sometimes') she said that she had long wanted to call but had not been sure which of us had settled in Malvern first. She of course had been connected with it longer but thought I had actually moved into The Mount before she and her husband had taken their present house. The responsibility for the first call had therefore been difficult to allocate.

I felt a trifle bewildered by these niceties and suggested a cup of tea. The addresses were then produced and served as a basis for the rest of the conversation. It was clear that the Genius had not overestimated her knowledge of German. I realized in fact that she was a woman of some culture who, whether or not she appreciated music and literature in themselves, certainly did not underrate their social value as subjects for discussion. But what remained as the dominant impression of the afternoon was the curious hesitancy of her speech and her almost incredible vagueness in regard to practical affairs. When she left she returned to the question of etiquette and said in her gracious, perhaps slightly condescending, way that she hoped I would waive formality and dine with them.

Excessive formality can hardly be said to have played a large part in my life so I waived it and accepted.

The Elgars were living at this time in Alexandra Road, Malvern Link. Their house, which is still standing and marked

with a memorial plate, was a semi-detached villa placed side-
ways to Alexandra Road in a kind of little square with a grass
plot in front. It was of a Victorian pattern that was then becoming somewhat démodé but has since acquired a certain period
appeal and was built of the local warm-coloured stone with
facings of a whitish brick. It was distinguished from the numberless Hill Views, Mon Repos, Chez Nous and Braemars by being
called 'Forli'. The name, chosen one may be sure by Alice
Elgar, referred not to the place but to Melozzo da Forli, the
painter of angel musicians, one of whom in the Church of S.s.
Apostoli at Rome so amusingly foreshadows a pose of modern
virtuoso conductors. Before the house across the strip of grass
was a magnificent view of the North Hill, the prow, as it were
of the Malverns.

When the evening of my visit arrived it brought a number of
fresh surprises of which the first was that my host and hostess
were were in full evening dress, something of a reproof to the
demi-toilette which I had supposed suitable to the occasion.
However they gave me a very kind welcome to their home and
showed me over it. It was the inside of the house that gave me
my second surprise that evening, for the furniture and decoration suggested a taste and a culture that could not have been
guessed from its somewhat surburban exterior.

The dining-room was on the right of the door as one entered,
the drawing-room, bigger because of its bay window, on the
left. The little study where so much music was to be scored was
on the first floor, at the back, to the left of the staircase. Each
contained a number of fine pieces of Indian carved furniture.
In the drawing-room were a few curios of which I remember a
case of scented Tonkin beans ('which always remind me of
Cranford,' said Mrs Elgar) and a collection of letters in Hindu
script encased in the beautiful silk bag with green tassels in
which they had journeyed from one prince to another.

I had never of course seen the Elgars together before and the
outstanding impression of that first evening was of the strange

disparity between them. So incompatible did they seem indeed that it was difficult to believe that they could be husband and wife. Mrs Elgar was wholly typical of the class to which she belonged. Like so many ladies of her time she had cultivated a number of rather indeterminate artistic pursuits in few of which she could be said to excel. She had the vagueness of manner which was then considered a mark of feminine refinement and all her utterances tended to float off into space. Even her most impressive pronouncements had to be finished by a wave of the hand rather than by anything so definite as the completion of a sentence.

Compared with his fluttering and perhaps rather affected wife the Genius seemed to belong to a world of cold realities, and indeed I had a feeling that a certain impatience with her affectation was making him rather more downright than he might otherwise have been. Thus when she complained that since her marriage she no longer had had access to the Army & Navy Stores he said abruptly, 'No; because I don't make it my business to kill my fellow men.'

I realized later that this remark was typical of a tendency, which he never outgrew, to say embarrassing things which were coloured by a hint of resentment. In this case the resentment, no doubt arose from the pain which had been caused him by people of superior social position generally and not by General Roberts in particular, whom of course he had never met. He seems indeed to have admired the General as something of a social model, and I always believed that it was this admiration that caused him increasingly to adopt the wholly unsuitable appearance of an army man in his own person. In the implied compliment to his wife and his father-in-law there was, I felt, as in many other of the minor details of Elgar's life, something profoundly touching.

Faced for the first time by this oddly matched couple I could not help wondering how they had harmonized their manifest differences of outlook and background and which of them it was whose standards had been imposed on the home. This last question was answered almost at once. Despite the softness of her voice and the gentleness of her manner there was a certain firmness, almost hardness, in the look of Mrs Elgar's china-blue eyes which convinced me that in the ordering of their home at any rate, it was she who drove the chariot even though her husband might occasionally flourish the whip. 'Forli' in short struck me as looking like the setting for an Anglo-Indian general's daughter rather than the workshop of a musician.

Whatever the relation between the Elgars may have been, however, one fact was evident and could not be questioned. This was that Mrs Elgar worshipped her husband with a devotion so absolute as to make her blind to his most obvious faults. It was clear from the outset that she did really believe his most trivial achievements to be works of genius and the germ was already present of an incapacity, unfortunate, because shared by her husband, to understand that hostile criticism of his music could be the result of anything but malice. I remember that when I was at 'Forli' on a later occasion she proudly drew my attention to a piece of poker-work—pyrography as it was called in the elegant language of the day—with which he had adorned the mantelpiece of his study. It represented the fire-motive from Walküre and seemed to me agreeably amateurish, yet she actually spoke of it with a kind of reverential awe. On that first night it was odd, after having listened to one of the Genius's confessions of frustration and failure, to hear the somewhat exaggerated terms in which his wife spoke, not merely of his talent but of his achievements—terms which rather surpassed the limits of good taste and indeed, as it seemed to me, of good sense.

An unusual couple, I thought; unusual but profoundly interesting.

Conversation over dinner, to which the Genius formally 'took me in', having formally offered me his arm, turned on a variety of subjects which showed the range of the Elgars'

interests. At that time I had not met many people in Malvern
who had much knowledge of, or interest in, foreign languages
or literature and it was pleasant to find that Mrs Elgar shared
my own taste for French and German. She was reading Suder-
man at the time and offered to lend me *Frau Sorge* which I did
not know and was glad to borrow. This led to another exciting
discovery for, when I asked her how she obtained such books
in Malvern, she told me of the London Library and its service
of book deliveries. She herself had become a life-member and I
decided then and there to follow her example.

The Genius, who took no particular interest in languages,
seemed in some danger of being crowded out of the conversation so, supposing that he might care to talk of his music, I
asked him some question about it. To my surprise he brushed
the subject aside and plunged into a dissertation on the game of
golf which he had recently taken up. He had not at that time
adopted the rather trying pose of not being interested in music
but I had a suspicion that this enthusiasm for golf was a trifle
artificial and something of a departure from his usual sincerity.
I felt, indeed, that golf appealed to him less as a game than as a
mark of a certain social status and that it represented an attempt
to live up to his wife's rather exacting standards. I found later
that, if this was so, the position could sometimes be reversed.
Not having had much leisure in his boyhood, the Genius had
never worked through some of the interests of childhood and
had retained them in adult life. One of these was kite-flying and I
have a vivid memory of seeing him running over Malvern Link
Common with his wife following as fast as her rather short
legs would carry her. 'Poor little lady,' said an old roadmender,
'He shouldn't make her run like that.'

The main subject of our evening's discussion was of course
the projected visit to Germany. For various reasons it was not
possible to travel out together—and in the end we did not stay
in the same house—but it was arranged that we should meet in
Munich and join forces for most of our outings. Dinner over,

we discussed our plans for the holiday at enormous length and the summer night had long fallen when I drove back across the Link Common, which looks today much as it did then, and through the rustling tree-lined roads to The Mount.

It had been a strange evening. But I felt that the Elgars would add enormously to the entertainment of the holiday and I dimly realized that a friendship had been formed which would play an ever-expanding part in my life.

8

Munich 1893

I believe that the Elgars, who left England earlier than Alice Davey and I, had begun with a plan of travelling to Munich by way of Ratisbon, where there were some Catholic music publishers, but in the end they spent their extra time at Garmisch in the Bavarian Highlands. They had been taken to Garmisch the year before by their friend Miss Baker (later to become the stepmother of Miss Dora Penny, the Dorabella of the *Enigma Variations*) and it was here that Edward saw the Schuhplatt'l dances which suggested his suite, *From the Bavarian Highlands*.

They arrived in Munich, where Alice Davey and I were already settled, on Thursday 17 August. We had of course an immense amount of news to exchange. The Elgars were full of their experiences at Garmisch, we of our journey up the Rhine, our rooms in the Theresienstrasse and of a visit to *Der Fliegender Holländer* so realistically staged that it had made us both feel sick. The holiday had brought out the most charming side of the Genius I had ever seen. At home I had usually met him in circumstances that seemed to make him feel ill at ease. He hated teaching and all the restraints of life in a provincial town yet could not shake himself clear of them. But here in Munich was a new-found freedom which gave an unaccustomed zest to life. It was clear from the outset that he intended to see and enjoy everything the holiday could offer, the black beer, the Church of the Theatines, the sausages, the Pinakothek

ESTABLISHED IN THE REIGN OF GEORGE III

ARMSTRONGS OF WORCESTER LTD.

Directors: A. R. Hyslop, W. C. Hyslop, N. E. Critchley

11, KING STREET
HEREFORD
TEL. 4084

13 AND 15 SANSOME WALK
WORCESTER
TEL. 22814

THE MANSE
CHURCH STREET
TEWKESBURY
TEL. 2494

3 Feb 1973

M

1. Waistcoat	8	00
1 Belt	1	10
	9	10

NO ENTRY

galleries, the Nymphenburg Palace with its famous rococo
decoration, above all the vast theatre where it was possible to
hear opera at prices which although raised for the Fest, were
still surprisingly moderate. On the night of the Elgars' arrival
we all went to *Die Meistersinger*.

The next day they came round from their rooms in the
Gluckstrasse to have tea with us and again I was struck with
the Genius's evident happiness. Like the rest of us, three
English people with little experience of Continental life, he had
found in Munich a world of new interests. He was delighted
with the Biedermeyer furniture of our rooms, the view from
the window, the Münchener Kind'l holding up his beer mug,
with the ancient tea-caddy and its green glass sugar box which
Frau Würmer, our landlady, had brought out in great excitement over the arrival of these English visitors and particularly
with a pointless but endearing little family joke which began
that afternoon and was to last for many years. A reference was
made to the Herrschaft and the Genius, not fully understanding
the meaning of the word, supposed it to refer to himself.

'This Herrschaft,' he said, 'is enjoying himself.'

In a quieter way Mrs Elgar also seemed to be happy. The
German culture was one with which she was clearly in deep
sympathy and I suspected that she felt more at home in Munich
than she would have done in many parts of England. Graciously
—for she was always gracious—she spoke in her excellent
German to Frau Würmer, complimenting her on her tea and
on the arrangement of her rooms. But it was noticed that, when
she referred to the Genius as 'mein Mann', the old Frau seemed
slightly taken aback.

The holiday gave me my first chance to observe Mrs Elgar
at all closely and I found her a very interesting study. In many
ways her behaviour towards the Genius was, as Frau Würmer
had hinted, that of the doting mother of a gifted son rather than
of a wife.

She had all the doting mother's fussiness and anxiety,

especially over his health, with the result that she sometimes irritated him. Moreover, as sons frequently do, he often refused to play the part for which she had cast him. In her immense— and indeed wholly self-sacrificing admiration for him—she seemed to feel that on every occasion he should act as general guide and mentor. Often of course he could live up to all that was expected, as, for instance, when he explained to us points in the musical texture of the operas. At other times one felt that he was having to pretend to know far more than he actually did to maintain this persona.

Sometimes, when he made an obvious mistake, it could be turned into a joke. There was one occasion when, having left us for an afternoon's exploration, he took one of the horse trams which amused him and, wishing to go to the end of the route, asked for the 'letzte Ruhe Platz'—to find himself put down at a cemetery. He told us of this adventure with great joy. But at other times things did not go so well, although one could not feel that the misunderstandings were the fault of either. The fact seemed to be that she expected him to behave like the men to whom she had been accustomed but that he, either not knowing what she wanted, or refusing to play the part required of him, would sulk or else ruin her comedy of manners with some gross piece of realism.

Thus, when she was expressing her admiration for Hans Sachs, the Genius deeply disgusted her by pointing out that a medieval shoemaker must have had coarse habits and had probably blown his nose between two fingers. This was really cruel since, as we all knew by this time, Mrs Elgar could only appreciate an idealized Sachs and would have regarded a real shoemaker as quite impossible. Again there was a similar incident in regard to Brahms for one day when she was expressing her enthusiasm for that master the Genius said, 'Yes Chickie, but don't forget that his favourite amusement in beer gardens was to take servant girls on his knee and tickle them.'

On such occasions she would somewhat naturally bristle with irritation and say, 'Really Eddu, I don't think we need dwell on that.'

I learned later that her invariable reaction to anything unpleasant was flatly to refuse to face it and to pretend that it did not exist.

But despite these little brushes and the irritation they sometimes caused, one impression remained from that Munich holiday and this was of Mrs Elgar's devotion to her husband. She had married him in defiance of the opinion of her friends and it was clear that she would stand by him whatever misfortune might befall. Hers was truly a great love.

It was a wonderful holiday. We saw all the sights of the city and I remember particularly Mrs Elgar's emotion in the National Museum when she looked on the blue and silver coronation robes of the unhappy young king, Ludwig of Bavaria who had befriended Wagner. And sometimes when it was so hot that one hesitated to cross the Ludwigstrasse because doing so meant leaving the shade of the high buildings, we would escape from the city and take a tram to the beautiful open-air baths at Schwabing where one could swim in the green waters of the Isar and try not to laugh at the *kolossal* figures of the Bavarian ladies engaged in the same pursuit. Their consumption of beer was said to be sixteen Krugs a day and I felt I could believe it, for they looked like enormous rubber balloons . . . Again when we felt like going farther afield there was the Starnberger See with its immense panoramic background of the Bavarian Alps. We saw the lakeside villa in which King Ludwig had been living when he met with his tragic and untimely death. . . .

The main concern of the holiday however was of course the Wagner Fest and this we took very seriously indeed. Three or four times a week we would go to the large Hoftheater to hear Herman Levi conduct one of the operas and, as this conductor, who was then approaching the end of his long career, was one

of the greatest Wagner interpreters—having in fact been entrusted with the first performance of *Parsifal* at Bayreuth—we
had the best possible introduction to this, as it then seemed,
revolutionary music.

It is difficult nowadays, when Wagner's music has become
completely absorbed, and, in fact, demoded, to realize the
electrifying effect it made when it was relatively new. To one
like myself whose experience was confined for the most part to
somewhat academic works, and the established classical
repertory, the music of Wagner, with its then seemingly complete disregard of the conventions of form and harmony, was
simply overwhelming. Its long melodic sweeps and its emancipation from small patterns made me think of the sea, the sea in
every conceivable mood, ranging from sunny calm to the
wildest tempest. This impression lasted throughout the holiday
and for many years after.

The season included most of the operas except *Parsifal* which
then and for many subsequent years was not played outside
Bayreuth. On the very night of the Elgars' arrival, as I have
said, we heard *Die Meistersinger* which delighted me for many
reasons, one of which was that I knew Beckmesser intimately,
having met with his type in the Kentish village in which I had
been born. The Genius had an immense admiration for the
part-writing of the quintet in the second act and in later years
I was often to be reminded of the evening, as he chose the
'Wach Auf' chorus for what would now be called the signature-
tune of the Worcestershire Philharmonic Society, who sang it
as a prelude to most of their meetings. Even later I was reminded of the evening again, for there is in the first movement
of Elgar's Second Symphony an unmistakeable, though doubtless unconscious, reference to a well-known phrase in the
opera.

On that first acquaintance, *The Ring* impressed me chiefly by
its interminable length and I was quite unable to understand
the Genius's enthusiasm, but *Tristan* was a shattering experi-

ence—Mrs Elgar, always deeply affected by romantic music, was the most touched—I remember that she admired the character of King Mark, a thoroughly 'nice' man—but on all of us the heavily erotic melodies worked such a spell as to make sleep impossible for the whole night.

The performances were arranged on the leisurely Bayreuth plan, which in England has been used at Glyndebourne, and began in the late afternoon. Then, after an act or so came the Grosse Pause in which one retired to the theatre restaurant to repair the emotional ravages made by the music with beer, Schnitzel, Semmel Brot and Sauerkraut, enlivened by an exchange of views on the performance. The real discussion, however, came after we left the theatre and adjourned to the Hofbrauhaus. There the whole opera would be reviewed, the playing criticized in detail and the technical means by which each effect had been obtained carefully analysed.

At that time the Genius had a great regard for Wagner but, unlike his wife, with whose schwärmerei he was always apt to be a little in conflict, he did not jettison his critical faculty. I remember that, despite his great admiration for the orchestration and the direction, he was very displeased with the coarse quality of the brass. The fact is that he had begun to understand very fully how the new music was put together and was realizing that he could convert this knowledge to his own use. Throughout the holiday he took copious notes of what he had heard and spent many hours over them at his rooms. In this he was encouraged by Mrs Elgar who, sometimes when we called to take him out, would put her finger to her lips and tell us he was too busy.

'My word,' said Alice Davey. 'Doesn't she keep him at it?'

She certainly did. Occasionally I felt that she kept him at it a little too much, though she was manifestly justified in the result. But I have to admit it was hard for us to be quite fair to her. We had gone to Munich for a holiday and were bent on enjoying ourselves. In these circumstances, Mrs Elgar's extremely serious attitude to the enterprise was apt to be as irritating to us as, no doubt, our frivolity was to her. Whether by taking an easier view of his work the Genius would in the end have benefited less I rather questioned for I always felt that his attitude to life was too tense and it seemed to me that, for example, his amusement at the absurd side of the operas was quite as good for him as were the musical hints which he picked up. This amusement was very great, so much so that one could hardly believe him to be the same man as the repressed and unhappy violin master I had known at The Mount. With his rather schoolboyish sense of fun he was immensely tickled by the all-too-generous proportions of the Rhinemaidens and, I think, always hoped that the ropes which supported them would give way. The unathletic gods, with the terrible clubs which they clumped on the stage, also pleased him, as did the final moment when Levi tottered on to the stage, a small stiff figure leading a vast soprano.

Mrs Elgar, whose admiration for everything German was proof against such assaults as these, saw no blemishes and was inclined to be hurt when our ribaldry brought them to her notice. I think she felt that our laughter infringed the seriousness and high purpose of the pilgrimage. It was therefore as well that she did not accompany us on what proved our most hilarious outing of all. It may be thought that, like Hollywood, the operas of Wagner are sufficiently absurd in themselves to be beyond the reach of parody but a parody of *Tannhäuser*, made seasonable by the Fest, was nevertheless being played at one of the other theatres in the city, and to this Alice Davey, the Genius and I went one night by way of relaxation. The humour —provided in the main by a Venus more huge even than a Wagner soprano—was not very subtle and perhaps our imperfect knowledge of German saved us a certain amount of embarrassment, but we laughed so immoderately that to Alice Davey (now Mrs Hurle-Cooke) the evening is still one of the outstanding memories of the holiday.

At the end of the month the Elgars had to return to England but Alice Davey and I, with a week still to spare, arranged to go for a short walking tour. Fired by the Elgars' account of Garmisch we decided to make this our first stage, following it by visits to Mittenwald, Zirl, Innsbruck and Salzburg. At Germisch we were anxious to see the Tyrolese dancers and, tired as we were, made our way to Die drei Möhren for dinner. There in the large dining-room we had our meal, while the dancers gave the entertainment that had inspired the Genius's as yet unwritten *Three Bavarian Dances*. Here again it may have been just as well that we did not understand the language completely but the spectacle, the vigorous hand-clapping over and under the legs and the twanging zithers, had a gaiety which I have never forgotten and which comes to mind every time I hear the *Three Bavarian Dances*. It may be worth mentioning, by the way, that the tunes Elgar used are original and not those heard at the inn, his object having been to recall the spirit of the dances and not the actual melodies that accompanied them.

The rest of the long walk is now a confused memory of villages to which the goats and cows came sedately down from the hillside in the evening, of rushing streams through little streets, of the deep cool pine forests and above all of the fiddle-making village of Mittenwald where we saw violins and 'cellos hanging out on the line like washing to dry in the sun and wind.

After the excitement of Munich we were both glad of a little peace, both inclined to be thoughtful rather than talkative. Of what passed through Alice Davey's mind I never learned for *qui sait que pensent les jeunes filles*? But, for myself, I was much concerned with the two friends who were now on their way to England. Why had the Genius been so much happier in Munich than in Malvern? No doubt most of us are happier on a holiday than when we are at work but in his case the difference seemed really disproportionate.

'Why,' he had said one day, 'can't one live this free and happy life in England?'

Did he ever think that question and its answer out to their logical conclusion? I suspect that he did not and that, had he done so, the answer would have surprised him.

9

The Three Choirs

It was one of Edward Elgar's peculiarities never to speak, even in the early days, of the teaching and playing by which he then really earned his living. This dislike for teaching—and, as he once rather amusingly told me, of schoolmistresses—took him to surprising lengths. Thus there was one occasion on which, having planned an open-air performance of *Comus*, I tried to make an arrangement of Arne's music (that of Lawes not having then been made available) for the forces we could muster. The Genius, whom I had not wished to trouble in this matter as I knew him to be busy, happened to call, and, seeing my poor efforts, roared with laughter, took the paper from me and showed me what was required, I was naturally very grateful and invited him to bring his wife to the performance.

At once I knew that I had said the wrong thing. It was not that he minded seeing an amateur performance but that he absolutely refused to appear in public in the detested role of a music-master. I was sorry that he did not come as the grave beauty of the children and the care with which they spoke Milton's lines made an impression that was long remembered.

It was not surprising therefore that, although the Genius was returning from Munich to play for the last time in the orchestra of the Three Choirs Festival at Worcester, he did not once mention it during the holiday. Yet the festivals were of the

greatest importance to his development as an artist and deserve
a place in any account of his career.

My own introduction to them came from another and
entirely unexpected source. In 1893 I had not, so far as I can
remember, ever heard of the Three Choirs Festivals. Living as
I did eight miles away from Worcester, I had not been much
drawn into the life of the city and, as it happened, the festivals
of 1891 and 1892 had taken place at Hereford and Gloucester
respectively.

One day, however, after my return from Munich, I was
standing on the platform of Foregate Street Station at
Worcester, after a morning's shopping, when a lady whom I
did not know, came to me and said, 'Are you musical?'

For the moment I wondered a little wildly if I were expected
to sing or dance but as she seemed quite serious, I composed
my features and admitted that I liked music. She then explained
that she had a ticket for the festival performance in the Cathedral
that afternoon but that, having attended most of the series, she
was suffering from musical indigestion and would like me to
accept the ticket.

I thanked her, took it and abandoning my train back to
Malvern, had some lunch and made my way to the Cathedral.

I had been vaguely aware that there was a good deal of social
activity in Worcester that day and had been told that the visitors
had come for the festival, but I had no conception as yet of its
local significance and was rather surprised to find the Cathedral
filled with a fashionable crowd of people listening to a full-scale
performance with chorus, orchestra and London principals of
one of the major oratorios. I remember that Albani was the
soprano.

This chance visit introduced me to an institution which in
those days at any rate was unique and of which I at once became
a devotee. The most obvious difference of this festival from any
other I had visited lay of course in the circumstances in which
one listened for, whereas at the average provincial festival the

performance would be given in some town hall, which might or might not be acoustically satisfactory, and in any case called up essentially worldly, and often non-musical, associations, at the Three Choirs meetings, held in turn in Gloucester, Worcester and Hereford, most of the music was heard in the cathedrals, in a setting which was certainly not wholly worldly and which had an acoustic quality that was rare, beautiful and strangely moving. To appreciate further more subtle differences one must glance briefly at the history of the movement.

The comparative proximity of the cities, which form roughly an equilateral triangle with sides about twenty-five miles long, was bound sooner or later to lead to experiments in combining the total forces of the cathedral choirs of the three, but what seems to have crystalized the meetings into their present form was the charitable object of assisting orphaned children of the poorer clergy of the three dioceses. A sermon on the subject is still preached at the opening services of each festival.

Since 1724, then, when the three choirs met in Gloucester for this purpose, there has been, with two breaks caused by the war of 1914 and that of 1939, an annual meeting which, taking place at each city in turn, has provided it with a triennial festival. The rotation in regard to geographical position is 'anti-clockwise' (Gloucester, Worcester, Hereford) and the sequence although broken by the 1914 war, was taken up again in 1920 at Worcester where the Festival would have been had there been no break. It is thus easy by a simple calculation to find where the meeting took place in any year up till 1939. By re-starting it at Hereford in 1946 however the promoters broke the ancient sequence which, if followed would have brought it to Worcester.

Although the festivals themselves date only from 1724, which even so, makes them the oldest of their kind in the country, the heritage of cathedral music with which they are associated links them with the earliest history of the Church. It is indeed, a fact that although for many years the Three Choirs

meetings developed into little more than Handel Festivals,
there was all the time, as I heard Sir Richard Terry point out, a
rich mine of pre-Reformation music in the cathedral libraries,
music which was ultimately exhumed, published and performed. One had thus at a Three Choirs Festival the feeling,
called up at no other such meeting, of association with a long
and continuous tradition of church music.

An institution which combined so many interests—musical,
ecclesiastical, charitable and, as will be seen, social—was inevitably torn by controversy. As the festivals grew in importance, so the musical forces employed were increased; local
choral societies were added to the choirs and larger orchestras
were called for. To accommodate this army of performers large
platforms had to be built in the cathedrals, to the undoubted
detriment of their dignity and the great annoyance of the more
conservative churchmen. Every year saw a revival in some
measure of the controversy that raged round this subject.
Nearly everyone felt that the staging was an abomination and
many were against its use. And while some held that nothing
should be sung but the offices of the Church and that all other
music, however delightful, was in the strict sense of the word,
profane, others claimed that music was the handmaid of religion
and that, since none but works of a religious character were
performed, the result must be edifying. A third point of view,
given to the present writers by a thoughtful church musician,
never seems to have occurred to anyone concerned. This is that,
since the acoustics of a cathedral are best suited to the volume
of sound produced by the traditional small body of voices singing in the choir or ambulatory, the introduction of large-scale
forces can only end in a blur of distortion. But compromise is
a large factor in the Church of England's composition and it
may be that all parties secretly shared the commonsense view
expressed in one of the preliminary sermons, namely that, as,
since the Reformation the clergy had been allowed to marry,
money was needed to provide for the orphans they sometimes

left, and that the Festivals supplied a pleasant and elevating means of earning that money.

The financial side of the institution was nevertheless a source of trouble. By an arrangement which, to the outsider, always seemed peculiarly absurd the festivals were financed by a group of guarantors—originally six in number, a clergyman and a layman from each diocese, but later more numerous—who agreed to make good any deficit but who were not allowed to share in any profit or even to carry it over to another, and possibly less successful, year. The whole of the profits were given to the Charity and as the expense of singers and orchestra constantly increased, the margin of security steadily dwindled. One of the most exasperating experiences of visitors was to find, after they had paid high prices for seats in a cathedral to which admission was technically free, that the stewards were waiting at the door, collecting for the charity which the seat money was supposed already to have supported.

Yet, with all their faults, The Three Choirs Festivals were an immense success, socially when I first knew them and later musically as well. This social success was due to a variety of causes. In order to appreciate it one must try to imagine a now remote day when neither radio nor gramophone existed and when travelling was not so easy or so general as it has since become. In such circumstances the performance locally of favourite works with the co-operation of such famous Metropolitan singers as Albani, Santley and Edward Lloyd was naturally an event of great interest. Another reason for popularity was the typically nineteenth-century English one that the festival enabled the most puritanical supporter to indulge in a four-days' orgy of musical entertainment under the pleasant pretext of supporting a charity. The country clergy and their families, many of whom would never have gone to the St James's Hall, turned up in droves. The local large houses also entertained for the festival with the same enthusiasm which they directed to the cause of shooting-parties and race-meetings.

The whole thing had a peculiarly English charm. The cathedral close concerned would be filled with a throng of gaily dressed people who knew no cares and seemed mainly concerned with the question of who was lunching with whom, how the shooting was going and whether the rain would spoil the Dean's garden party. Amongst these, as distinct as currants in pastry, stalked the musicians, a race apart with their strange hats and stranger hair. By 1893 musicians were no longer regarded necessarily as vagabonds and the most distinguished of them were even invited to a few social functions but as yet they had not become the lions of the occasion. Edward Elgar himself told me of what was possibly the most striking contrast of all. He remembered that in 1884 there suddenly appeared amongst those placidly polite English faces the fierce peasant's jowl of Antonin Dvórak who had come to conduct his *Stabat Mater*. His strange figure striding down Foregate Street seemed almost as much out of place in Worcester as did his fervent Slavonic music when heard amidst the sedate hymn-tunes of the cantatas then being written for the festivals by English composers.

On the side of solid musical achievement the value of the festivals is harder to assess. The difficult financial arrangement necessitated—as Dr Colles pointed out in *Grove's Dictionary*—a bid for popularity and it has to be admitted that, with one or two notable exceptions, the works sung followed, rather than led, public taste. New music was certainly produced but it was chosen by very conservative standards and for every *Messiah* or *Elijah* discovered there were countless cantatas on Biblical subjects by cathedral organists, teachers of harmony and other not very highly inspired professional musicians, which, having been sung once, were thankfully dropped for ever. It was said that nearly every line of the Bible was ultimately used for some cantata or other—except of course the genealogical tables.

Towards the end of the nineteenth century the programmes,

having passed through many phases, with high-lights provided at different times by Handel, S. S. Wesley and Mendelssohn, had sunk in the main to a rather depressing level of dulness. There was a Sunday service and then, beginning on the Tuesday, four days of drearily conventional music in the cathedral with a couple of secular concerts in the Shire Hall. Sandwiched between *Elijah*, which usually opened the Festival, and *Messiah* which closed it, came a waste of ephemeral works which greatly cooled the interest. The only hope of variety lay in the circumstances of performance, the interpretation and the weather. Hereford was—and is—the most attractive of the three cities; Gloucester, where on account of some acoustic quality the whole cathedral seemed to become itself an instrument was musically the most satisfactory; Worcester, in many ways less pleasant than the others, ultimately acquired the interest of having been most closely associated with Edward Elgar. Interpretation did not greatly vary although it was always mainly in the hands of the organist at whose particular cathedral the festival took place and the weather thus added the greatest variety of all. There was a tradition that it was always fine for Gloucester and wet for Worcester.

Some touch of novelty had long been needed and it was eventually provided, not by Elgar, but by Parry. The son of a wealthy Gloucestershire landowner and popular with the class who supported the festival, he was the first Englishman of recent times to contribute a work found worthy of repetition. This was *Prometheus Unbound* which, produced at Gloucester in 1886, at once became popular. It may be that today few would endorse Hadow's enthusiastic claim that English music had at last come into its own and come with a masterpiece in its hand but there is no doubt that a new and welcome departure had been made. Like others of its kind, the revolution was sometimes to go a little too far. Sir Thomas Beecham recalls an occasion when Delius conducted one of his *Dance Rhapsodies* with rather unexpected results, the part of the bass-bassoonist

having been filled by a young and inexperienced woman who
completely destroyed the gravity of many of the audience by
sounds which suggested 'the painful endeavour of an anguished
mother-duck to effect speedy evacuation of an abnormally large-
sized egg'. And others will remember how the Dean and
Chapter shrivelled into their surplices with horror when a
sturdy soprano singing a passage set by Bantock from the *Song
of Solomon*, suddenly screamed through the cathedral, 'Let him
kiss me with the kisses of his mouth'. But in general a great and
overdue improvement had been made. Henceforth the British
composer who had something to say was as sure of a hearing as
the dreary spinners of harmonic and contrapuntal patterns who
had hitherto held the field.

This, then, was the stage which was set for Edward Elgar to
tread. True to form it did not—as he was afterwards bitterly to
complain—welcome him very readily. Although most of his
major works were in the end performed at the festivals with a
sort of religious fervour, very few were given there for the first
time. The chief exception was the overture, *Froissart* (Worcester
1890) and this was ruined by the acoustics of the Shire Hall.

Yet it was on this stage that he was to make his most
characteristic appearances. He had often—and justly—spoken
contemptuously of the Festivals and of those who wrote for
them, yet he himself was to become the lion of the meetings
and his works were to take in them the place formerly occupied
by those of Handel.

10

Turning Point

The stage was set but in 1893 Elgar was still amongst the supernumeraries and nowhere near to playing a leading part. He had returned from Munich more than ever convinced that he had it in him to write great music but equally convinced, alas, that no one wanted his 'stuff'. I do not think that the deep-rooted and destructive sense of grievance from which he was to suffer throughout the rest of his life can be attributed wholly to those dreary years of waiting for the first glimmerings of widespread recognition. It seems far more likely that the grievance originated much earlier in the circumstances of his home life, but there is no doubt that it was fed by the years of waiting until it began to develop into something like persecution mania. It was during those years that he began openly to admit to the belief that there were malignant forces actually working against his success, and so firmly did the conviction take root that, to the end of his life when his music was being played all over the world he could and, as we shall see, did complain that nobody wanted it.

Dr Percy Scholes has truly said that it was the English festival system that gave Elgar his first opportunity. And indeed this system was, in the last years of the nineteenth century, almost the only hope of a composer who needed to make money. But there were two kinds of festival and although Elgar was ultimately successful at those typified by the meeting of the

Three Choirs and by the Birmingham Triennial Festival, many of his earliest successes arose in connection with what were in reality choral competitions.

Ever since 1885, when Miss Wakefield had founded her quartet competitions at Kendal, there had been a steady increase in the movement and in the demand for works which could be used at the hundreds of new centres which were being opened. The part songs which Elgar was now beginning to write, published by Novello, the chief purveyors of this kind of music, were exactly what was wanted and they sold in large quantities. The secret of their appeal was that, far more than the old classical choruses, they enabled judges to assess the musicianship of the competing conductors and their teams. For Elgar, thinking, as was his wont, instrumentally rather than chorally, really orchestrated his voices and expected a subtlety in the handling of the parts that needed skill and care in performance. A choir that could shout its way cheerfully through the *Hallelujah Chorus* might make a very poor showing indeed with *My Love Dwelt in a Northern Land*.

To this period belong many of his most famous part songs. In addition to the setting of Andrew Lang's words—which led to an acrimonious dispute with Lang, who failed to appreciate that his poem would owe its immortality to Elgar's wings—he wrote *Fly Singing Bird, The Snow,* and *Oh Happy Eyes.* One of our most regular amusements at this time was to look through the lists of test pieces set for the competition festivals. Every Elgar work chosen meant of course an increase not only in the sales but in the spread of his fame.

His attempt to write solo songs of the ballad variety, however, was noticeably less successful. T. F. Dunhill said in his assessment of Elgar's work that he found it 'almost unbelievable that a composer of such power and distinction should have been willing to attach his name to productions like *After, The Pipes of Pan. Come Gentle Night* and *Pleading.*' Some of them he considered scarcely distinguishable from pot-boilers turned out by baser English composers in the days of ballad concerts.

In Elgar's defence it must be pointed out that he had his living to earn and that, having to sell what publishers would buy, he had to make settings of puerile verses. He himself had a great contempt for composers who wrote pot-boilers and sometimes threatened to enter the market against them. It never occurred to him that since his musical imagination was, as Hubert Foss said after his death, 'more productive of musical texture than of actual musical ideas' he was ill-equipped to compete against the mere spinners of tunes and that his minor efforts in song-writing, in consequence, were bound to be noticeably less satisfying than theirs. He was also handicapped by a curious failure to appreciate the words he chose to set. His friend Ernest Newman, who had from the first an immense admiration for Elgar's genius, repeatedly drew attention, more one imagines in sorrow than in anger, to the weakness of Elgar's settings which seemed always to follow the line-shape instead of the meaning. It was all to no purpose. Again and again songs would appear—such as the setting of A. C. Benson's *Speak Music*—in which the rhythm of the words was completely broken and remoulded to fit music with a different metrical pattern.

But if Elgar's deafness to the poetry of words accounts for the ineptitude of his settings, it does not explain the fact that his songs seemed to contain most of his worst melodies. His own explanation of inspiration made to R. J. Buckley was, 'My theory is that there is music in the air and that you just take as much as you require.' This is as good a theory perhaps as any other, suggesting as it does that the composer's subjects, like the painter's, are everywhere for the taking. But Elgar omitted to mention—perhaps because he did not fully realize—the necessity of selection. No doubt he had a selective faculty of some kind but it seems to have been unconscious and to have functioned only when he was inspired by some worthy end.

In writing shop-ballads he was further handicapped by the

fact that he was catering for the two media with which he was least in sympathy, the pianoforte and the human voice. In these circumstances inspiration was dead indeed, the selective process failed him and he could blandly produce tunes which would have been rejected as unworthy by such composers as Stephen Adams and Sanderson. Perhaps the low ebb, so far as songs that are still heard are concerned, was reached with a ballad called *Pleading*, which is marked as Elgarian by the characteristic drop from the supertonic to the submediant (also used in *Land of Hope and Glory*), but which touches a depth of banality that is almost incredible.

When Elgar did occasionally conceive an idea that fitted the genius of the piano, inspiration came and flourished. In *The Shepherd's Song* the piano accompaniment does vividly suggest the movement of driven sheep, a fact of which an orchestrator who subsequently scored it seems wholly to have overlooked. And again when the hated piano could be replaced by an orchestra, as in *Sea Pictures* which, though far from being a great work has fine moments, his imagination took fire and gave us something memorable.

In parenthesis one may point out that his contempt for the piano and the voice led to a rather amusing inconsistency. Elgar was one of the most ruthless critics of those composers who first wrote a work in piano score and then clothed it in orchestral colours and whose orchestration was always hampered by their ignorance of what each instrument could comfortably do. Again and again he has pointed out to me passages in the works of these 'keyboard composers' in which the trombones or horns had been given passages that were nearly unplayable.

'Why don't these people learn to appreciate the nature of the instruments they write for?' he would complain.

It was a just complaint and one which, so far as orchestral instruments were concerned, could not be levelled at him. Yet when it came to writing for the voice and piano he was almost as bad a sinner as the amateur orchestrators. Mr Dunhill has pointed out the 'quite earnest ineffectiveness' of the piano writing at the beginning of the quintet, op. 84, and one has only to glance at any of the arrangements, made by Elgar himself, of his orchestral works, such as, for instance, *Dream Children*, to realize how complete was his own failure to appreciate the true nature of the piano.

At the beginning of 1894 Elgar developed a quinsy which put a stop to any kind of work for some weeks. It was one of a number of illnesses to which he seemed to have been tending for some time. Mrs Elgar's deep devotion to her husband and desire to shield him from every possible adverse influence sometimes resulted in what seemed to me far too much fuss about quite trifling, and indeed imaginary ailments, but, as often happened in such circumstances the imaginary ailments, aggravated in this case by a sense of grievance over non-recognition, gave way to real ones of which the quinsy was a distressing example. During this time his friends would send him all kinds of delicacies. My own contribution was two dozen oysters which I bought one day in Worcester. I had merely guessed that he liked oysters but the guess proved to be right.

So far as public recognition was concerned the first turning point was now almost within sight. The part songs were really beginning to sell. Novello's accepted and paid for *Oh Happy Eyes* on March 23. In April *Sursum Corda* for strings, brasses and organ was performed at a special service in Worcester Cathedral and *The Black Knight* was sung at Hereford in November and Walsall in December. And in the meantime a new work had been conceived.

Actually there were several. A cantata called *The Banner of St George* written to celebrate the Diamond Jubilee of Queen Victoria in 1897 (and no more successful than is usual with such *pièces d'occasion*), an organ sonata and the *Scenes from the Bavarian Highlands* were all on the stocks at much the same time, but the really important work now beginning also to take shape was one which at first was known simply as *Sagas*. This slowly developed as a sort of background to the others and was not completed till the April of 1896.

Before then much else had happened. The organ sonata, composed specially for the visit to Worcester Cathedral of some American organists was played by a friend of Elgar's whose habits, for all his distinction as a musician, were, to put it mildly, erratic. (He had on one occasion been engaged to spend a day examining the girls at The Mount and had neither turned up nor sent any explanation.) His performance of the sonata showed that he had either not learned it or else had celebrated the event unwisely for he made a terrible mess of poor Elgar's work. I was present at this débacle and commiserated with the Genius. But with a splendid flash of loyalty he refused to blame the murderer who, he said, had not had time thoroughly to study the victim.

Mr R. Nettel, whose two books, *Music in the Five Towns* and *Ordeal by Music*, contain valuable and original character sketches of the Elgar of those days, points out that he 'is this country's most obvious example of the fallacy that a prophet is without honour in his own country' and goes on to show that 'it was the people among whom he lived who encouraged the young Elgar to compose music'. After drawing attention to the sad picture of Elgar and his newly-married wife settling hopefully in London and being refused a hearing by both publishing houses and impresarios, Mr Nettel says, 'To Worcester, Hereford, Gloucester and Birmingham on the other hand, cities that had known him from a boy, Elgar was acceptable as a serious composer and given his chance.'

This is of course true. But what is even more important is Mr Nettel's reminder that much of the credit for spreading Elgar's fame among his own people in the Midlands was due to a friend whom most of the biographers have completely ignored. This was Dr Swinnerton Heap, a musician of very great attainments who, after a brilliant studentship—he won the Mendelssohn Scholarship and at Leipzig, studied pianoforte under Moscheles in addition to composition, organ and solo singing—chose to lavish his gifts on the Midlands where he had been born. In a short time Heap was wielding an immense influence. He conducted the Birmingham Philharmonic Union, and founded similar societies in all the towns he visited on his weekly itinerary as a music teacher, which included Malvern, Leamington, Walsall, Wolverhampton and Stoke-on-Trent as well as Birmingham.

It was through the agency of this indefatigable organizer of festival choirs that *The Black Knight* was sung in 1895 at Wolverhampton and it was he who first secured for Elgar the commission for a large-scale choral work. At that time Elgar had had some immediately local successes in Birmingham and the Three Choirs area but his fame had hardly spread beyond. A cantata for which I had suggested the name of *Lux Christi* had been accepted for the Worcester Festival but, although this was sure to win a certain amount of attention from London, it was Dr Heap's offer that enabled him to take his first real step forward as a festival composer. The story of that commission is typical of much that was to follow and especially of Elgar's relations with those who sought to help him.

The cantata which had first been known as *Sagas* was a setting for chorus and orchestra of scenes from the saga of *King Olaf* by Longfellow. I confess that my heart sank when I realized that Longfellow was once more to serve as librettist and my hopes were not encouraged by a study of the poem. *Olaf* is a wretchedly muddled story in which there is neither consistency of character nor unity of plot. It is always difficult enough to follow the plot of any cantata but when we are asked to believe that the three soloists are skalds or bards who stand round and tell the story, occasionally impersonating various characters, the confusion becomes hopeless. The fact that the soprano and bass each represent more than one person, makes it impossible for the listener to know at any moment who is supposed to be speaking and indeed after hearing it a good many times with the score I have only the vaguest idea as to what it is all about.

Elgar himself seems to have had doubts of Longfellow's ability to tell the story for he employed a rather pompous friend, a retired Indian civil servant named Acworth to fill in a few of the gaps. Mr Acworth's muse may not have been very distinguished but she compared favourably enough with Longfellow's.

> King Olaf's dragons take the sea
> The piping south wind drives them fast,
> The shields dip deep upon the lee,
> The white sails strain on every mast.

So wrote Mr Acworth of Olaf's death and the lines have a dignity strangely wanting in Longfellow's closing stanza with its delightful anticipation of the patent medicine style—

> A strain of music ends the tale,
> A low, monotonous, funeral wail,
> That with its cadence wild and sweet,
> Makes the long saga more complete.

Not all the lines are as feeble as these. It is evident indeed that some of the others, having a certain pictorial quality, might well inspire a composer with Elgar's gifts for musical illustration but, taken as a whole they do seem to suggest a curious deafness to verbal values in the composer who could choose them for a libretto. That he himself was not conscious of their weakness is proved I think by the extent to which he was fascinated by what may be called the Longfellow movement. Indeed he asked me to read it up for him and I spent a fortnight of my holidays in the British Museum Library studying the literary group who had surrounded Longfellow at Cambridge, Massachusetts, and made a sheaf of notes on the subject.

King Olaf was the first of Elgar's works with which I had

been personally closely concerned and I was able to watch a
sequence of moods that was to be repeated with nearly every
work I watched him compose. To begin with there would be a
period of great exaltation over the conception of the work and
the commission of the Festival Committee. This was always
followed by a period of black despair over the intractability of
the material and the utter impossibility of ever getting it into a
satisfactory shape. An immense amount of encouragement,
accompanied by assurances that he was the only person able to
do it and reminders that it must at all costs be done, had now
to be expended in order to shift him into the next phase which
was one of increasing hope and enthusiasm. Tunes, contrapuntal patterns and sequences had begun to suggest themselves for various sections of the work and would start to build
up almost without his conscious control into something like
the completed whole. He did not begin at page one and write
the work in the order in which it would be played. He was
more likely to start with a finale and build up each section in
reverse order until he reached the opening. But more generally
he wrote as fancy and the inspiration of this or that passage of
the libretto dictated.

He would now begin to be comparatively happy; his pupils,
always the principal sufferers during the period of gestation,
began to retire into the grateful shade of his disregard and he
would excitedly play me thematic scraps and chord-progressions
with which he proposed to illustrate points in the text of the
cantata.

'What do you think of this for Gudrun?' he would say, or,
'This is the Challenge of Thor.'

It was not always easy to grasp from these snippets the
magnificent effect which he himself could hear in his mind's
ear and which would be fully realized in performance but when
he played me the now-famous *As Torrents in Summer* I knew
that he had written an ending to his cantata which, whatever
the defects of the stumbling ill-told story, would send his

audience away with a memorable tune ringing in their ears.

The happiness of composing a work was in sharp contrast to the rage, depression and disgust which were usually aroused by the first performance. The nervous strain of writing left him ill able to cope with the practical problems which arose, and the result was that he was always miserable when this final stage was reached. The soloists were vain and capricious, the choir mulish and stupid and the committee a collection of parsimonious tradesmen without the most elementary appreciation of musical requirements.

The commission for *Olaf* came from the committee of the North Staffordshire Festival which was to be held at Hanley and it caused us the greatest excitement. Here was not only an offer to perform the work but an engagement to conduct it. There were telegrams to send and receive, visits to Hanley for conferences with the Festival Committee and endless correspondence both with them and with Novello's who were publishing the work. It is more than doubtful however whether this commission would have been given but for the insistence of Dr Heap, as Mr Nettel tells us that the committee had never heard any work of Elgar's and had several others under consideration. That Dr Heap had an immense admiration for Elgar's work is confirmed by another witness for Mr George Woodhouse, who originally studied under Dr Heap, told the present writers that when as a young man he expressed a great admiration for Grieg, Heap replied, 'Yes, but the composer who in years to come will stand head and shoulders above Grieg is Edward Elgar.'

It might therefore be supposed that Elgar would feel a deep debt of gratitude to his friend and that this gratitude would be recorded in his papers and ultimately mentioned by his biographers few of whom could write of the early days from personal observation. But actually events took a very different course.

I was not able to attend the first performance of *King Olaf*, as

it was given on 13 October (1896) in the middle of the autumn
term, and Hanley, although less than 100 miles away was not
then a very easy day's trip from Malvern. What I gathered however, was that the freshness of Elgar's music had triumphed
over the story and had made what is nowadays called a smash-
hit. The modest little *Lux Christi* which had been produced a
month before at the Worcester Three Choirs Festival was completely overshadowed. It was not merely that Hanley had been
impressed, though there were many signs of Elgar's having
been lionized—sometimes a little oddly as when the potters
designed a special mug to commemorate the occasion. The
important point was the effect made on the London press. Much
of what was written was trivial but the critic of the *Athenaeum*,
a responsible and perceptive musician whose opinion was worth
having, shrewdly pointed out that the orchestration was worthy
of Wagner. This was praise indeed and it had its effect. Elgar
had arrived and henceforth would begin to taste the sweets of
success.

His reaction was rather strange. He sent me a note from
Hanley in which he said 'Truly success is harder to bear than
adversity', and when he returned to Malvern and came to see
me I had a feeling that he was overwhelmed and a little
frightened. I have always supposed that he had had a sudden
glimpse of what might be expected of him but it is clear from
Mr R. Nettel's *Ordeal by Music* published in 1945 that there was
another more simple reason.

Quoting from the experience of Mr Havergal Brian, the
composer, who was present, Mr Nettel tells us that the success
of *King Olaf* was only won after it had trembled very dangerously
in the balance. Edward Lloyd, the tenor who was to sing the
name-part failed 'through a train error' to appear at the final
rehearsal. As a result there was an awkward moment in 'And
King Olaf heard the cry' when Elgar, already nervous and
fidgety, began to lose grip. The situation was only saved by the
prompt action of the leader of the orchestra, Willy Hess, who

actually 'jumped to his feet and straightened the thing out by
his presence and his bow.'

This incredible scene, of which no mention was ever made
to me, must have been very unnerving to the composer-
conductor already overwrought by the anxiety of the occasion,
and it had an unfortunate result. For, without perhaps carefully
analysing the causes of the accident, Elgar turned against Dr
Swinnerton Heap and blamed him for Lloyd's failure to appear
at the rehearsal. It is difficult not to sympathize with Elgar's
exasperation but he made a mistake in venting it on the one
man in Hanley to whom he really owed the production of his
work. Heap was very naturally deeply injured by this in-
gratitude and the breach was never healed.

But however much Elgar's nerve may have been shaken by
this incident he pulled himself together and a few weeks later
took the score to August Manns, an elderly German conductor
whose concerts at the Crystal Palace had introduced many new
works to the London public. Manns received him kindly,
looked over the score and promised a performance, which was
in fact given on 3 April of the next year—1897.

London was much more accessible than Hanley, the end of
the spring term was at hand and I took a party of pupils to the
Palace for the Concert.

11

Some Friendships

Long before the production of *King Olaf* in 1896, I had begun to
see Alice and Edward Elgar against a background of friends
and acquaintances, many of whom were to exert a profound
influence on the Elgars' lives as well as on my own. An Elgar
circle as such never existed and it is significant that the *Enigma
Variations*, a set of musical portraits dedicated to 'my friends
pictured within,' depicts a group of people hardly any one of
whom, other than Alice and Edward, can have known all the
others. In those years the Elgars were not very happily placed
for forming friendships. The rigid ideas of caste which Alice
had naturally taken over from her Anglo-Indian father made
many of Edward's friends unacceptable to her—she hardly ever
visited the old Elgars at their music shop—and a good many
of her own friends had cut her for marrying a man who, in their
pathetically limited view, was 'unsuitable'. A number of them
were faithful, however, and as time went on others began to
realize that in marrying Edward she had not instantly degraded
herself to the despised status of a tradesman's wife.

Amongst those whose loyalty never wavered for one moment
was what may be called the Hasfield Court group. The squire
of Hasfield was a Mr W. M. Baker who used generally to give
a house-party for the Three Choirs Festival when it took place
at Gloucester. But, although Mr Baker ultimately figured in the
Enigma Variations portrait gallery and his sister and wife did

not, it was they to whom the Elgars owed most. Mrs Baker was far more bohemian in taste than most of Alice's friends and probably had some understanding of Edward's ambitions. Miss Baker, the sister, however, really went out of her way to help and befriend the Elgars. A woman of great personal charm and character, she had known Alice for many years and, so far from frowning on the marriage, gave it every encouragement. It was she who in 1892 first took the Elgars to Garmisch in Bavaria and to the German opera-houses where Edward heard *Tristan*. Miss Baker ultimately became the second wife of the Rev Alfred Penny of Wolverhampton and was thus able to ask them to the pseudo-Elizabethan rectory there where they cemented a further friendship with Mr Penny's daughter by his first marriage. Dora Penny was one of the youngest of the Elgars' friends and used often to stay with them in Malvern. Her record of those visits, first published in 1936, gives an amusingly vivid account of the more boisterous and facetious side of Edward's character and is of great value as one of the very few pieces of independent observation of his behaviour at that time. For many years she served voluntarily as what Edward called Keeper of the Archives (actually collator and arranger of press-cuttings) a post which I myself was asked to take over after her marriage to Mr Richard Powell.

Another family who were unswervingly loyal lived closer at hand—in fact in Graham Road, Malvern, between The Mount and 'Forli'. The Fittons, whose ancestors had been related to Lady Mary Fitton, the 'dark lady' of Shakespeare's sonnets, were perhaps the most cultured and, to me, the most interesting members of the local society of that time. Musically alone they were an immense asset for they provided amongst themselves a thoroughly competent piano quartet, but their capacity for wise and understanding friendship was an even more valuable gift. Old Mrs Fitton, who lived to be nearly 100 years old, was a brilliant pianist and an exceptionally acute observer of human nature. Despite her affection for the Elgars, she managed to preserve a detachment which enabled her not only to see them steadily and whole, but to forecast with astonishing accuracy, how they would behave in any situation that might arise. Her daughter Isabel became one of my most valued friends.

A third group who deserve mention here lived at Sherridge, a pleasant eighteenth-century house standing in a small park to the north west of the hills. The Norburys were an old family who, though not so gifted as the Fittons, also took an intelligent interest in music and joined in many local efforts to make it. Miss Winifred Norbury retained Edward's friendship to the end of his life.

Edward's own friends of that time were mostly connected with music but there were two exceptions. A. Troyte Griffith was a Malvern architect whose office was in the Abbey gateway. The round shape of his head had earned him the nick-name of Ninepin but he always reminded me of a big dog. There was something doglike in his quiet admiration of Edward and also in the readiness with which, dressed in Harris tweeds with a mustard-coloured tie, he followed him on long tramps round the Malvern countryside. Troyte was not in the least musical but he gradually acquired an interest in music from the association with Edward and even undertook the management of a success-ful series of concerts. A somewhat stolid man in outward appear-ance, the Ninepin was by no means wooden-headed. He designed the church which stands on Malvern Common and recorded his love for the hills in a series of water-colours, three delicate and beautiful examples of which were owned by Mrs Elgar Blake.

The other non-musical friend was Dr Grindrod, a mental specialist who numbered Aubrey Beardsley among his patients. Dr Grindrod lived at the Wyche, one of the passes through the Malvern Hills, and he too was always ready to go for long walks. A gifted amateur photographer, he took the portrait of Edward which came nearer than any other to capturing his character.

The friends associated with Edward's musical interest were, as might be expected, something of an assortment, some of whom were not exactly cast by nature for parts in the Malvern comedy. Of these musical friends the first, a boyhood companion indeed, was Hubert Leicester. As a young man he had played the flute in the Elgars' family ensemble and although the friendship was for many years not particularly fervent, it lasted for the whole of Edward's life. When indeed, loaded with honours, Edward finally returned to Worcester to live in 1929, Mr Leicester, who had achieved civic distinction there, became, I believe, one of his most regular visitors.

The friendship with Dr Swinnerton Heap was not, as we have seen, so long-lived, but it led to another which was of the greatest importance. Edward's relations with his publishers had never been particularly happy. He had sold the early *Salut d'Amour* for a few pounds to Schott & Co, in 1889, and had thus received practically no share in the fortune it was supposed to have earned. We may or may not agree with Mr R. Nettel that 'in common with a great many other composers, Elgar did not hesitate to regard as an enemy anyone who did not behave exactly as he wished' but there is no doubt that he was difficult and suspicious—sometimes with good reason—over the publication of his subsequent work. There had been friction with Novello's over his description of *The Black Knight* as a symphony for chorus and orchestra, and *King Olaf*, which he had planned as a continuous work with orchestral interludes connecting the choral passages, had been broken up into a series of disjointed sections purely to satisfy the whims of the departmental chief who saw it through the press. A change was clearly overdue and Novello's handed the management of Edward's succeeding works to their reader, August Jaeger.

Edward used to bring most of the friends who visited him at Malvern to see me at The Mount but I first met Mr Jaeger at a little hotel in Manchester Square, London, where the Elgars happened to be staying. He was a lovable but rather typically commonplace little German with a very large head and a guttural accent and it was apparent from the outset that he was not only deeply impressed with Edward's ability but inclined to worship him as a hero. If this was the man who was to handle Edward's work at Novello's in future, I felt that we could look forward to an easier passage.

And indeed his value to Edward became very great. As editor of *The Musical Times* and reader to Novello's he wielded a great power and, although he often irritated—in fact infuriated—Edward by criticism of points of detail, there is no doubt that he managed to lubricate a relation between composer and publishers which without his patient intervention would have been anything but smooth. His appearance in *Grove's Dictionary* is avowedly due to the help he gave in advancing the reputation of Edward's early work, but, much as I admired him, I have often wondered whether his influence was quite as beneficial as is usually supposed.

At that time, although an English school was arising, musical opinion in this country was largely dictated by Germans, Jewish and otherwise, and it was these people who, if they did not discover, were most successful in popularising Edward's music. So much was Mr Jaeger's encouragement valued indeed that he once complained to me that Alice was perpetually writing to ask him to stir Edward into fresh activity. This championship by Germans did not, as Mr Nettel points out, help Edward's cause with the English school but there was an even more serious disadvantage. For Edward's genius, much as its development may have owed to the example of Wagner and Brahms, was not really Teutonic in spirit but akin rather, even in some of its faults, to that of César Franck and should not have been constantly assessed by exclusively German standards. One may therefore be a little doubtful of the value of a mentor whose principal requirement of a work of genius was that it should move him to tears.

Nevertheless poor little Mr Jaeger was probably the most faithful friend Edward ever had and when he died in 1909, racked by the consumptive cough which I had noticed with concern at our first meeting, he had probably done more for his hero's music than anyone else before or since.

Another of Edward's friends who fitted even more oddly (and much more frequently) into the Malvern scene was the exuberant Herr Ettling.

Herr Ettling was an extraordinary figure, stout, very ugly and short-sighted with strong magnifying spectacles. He was always jingling sovereigns in his trouser pockets. As his main occupation he was a traveller in Rhenish and other German wines and used to stay at the Palace Hotel (now Malvern Girls' College) near the station. But he had many other interests and in a Teutonic way combined some of the characteristics of Figaro and Autolycus. He loved playing the timpani—which he did extremely capably—could entertain the children, grown up and otherwise, with conjuring tricks, and was a sort of confidential agent who could obtain or dispose of anything or everything. Edward, who had seen *Parsifal* in 1892, called him 'Uncle Klingsor' but it was as a pedlar at a German fair in the Middle Ages that Herr Ettling would really have been in his element.

To Alice and Edward Elgar he was an indispensable embarrassment since, while he had, like so many foreigners, not the slightest feeling for the English social distinctions that were so dear to Malvern, and was, in fact, 'quite impossible' he knew a large number of influential musical people to whom Edward was glad to be introduced. It was through him indeed—or so he claimed—that the Elgars were invited to Edward Speyer's house, Ridgehurst at Shenley, which then, and for many subsequent years was a sort of musicians' Mecca. But to my German governess, a woman trained in the best aristocratic traditions, Herr Ettling was anathema and it distressed her that we should accept him on any social terms whatever.

'He is nothing but a gutter-merchant,' she said.

Of a third important friend, also German, it is difficult for me to speak as he rarely came to Malvern. Since he undoubtedly had an important influence, however, he should be mentioned. This was A. E. Rodewald, a Liverpool merchant of considerable means who was an amateur and patron of music and something of a conductor. I have always remembered the glow with which Edward told me of a meeting at Bettws-y-Coed at Mr Rodewald's house with Ernest Newman. The talk had turned on, among other subjects, Caroline poetry and it made a deep impression. For once Edward felt that he had been fully and sympathetically understood.

12

The Worcestershire Philharmonic Society

The production of *King Olaf* at Hanley seemed the signal for a general outburst of Edward's works all over the country. Up till this time few if any of them had been heard outside of the Three Choirs–Birmingham area but in 1897 *Olaf* was given at the Crystal Palace, Bishop Auckland, Liverpool and Camberwell; some of the songs were sung by Charles Phillips at the St James's Hall, *The Banner of St George* appeared and the *Imperial March*, also composed in honour of Queen Victoria's Diamond Jubilee, was played at both Queen's Hall and the Albert Hall in addition to the performances at a State Concert by command of the Queen. Wider recognition, it was evident, was on the way.

It was at this point that Edward made a very painful discovery regarding musical economics. He found that, because the great public which supported music had always valued the executant far above the composer, the latter received only the tiniest proportion of the price that was paid for musical performance, if indeed any proportion at all. He thus had the humiliating experience of being expected to write music for next to no financial return while those who performed it received fees that were often princely. The situation, exasperating to any composer, was doubly so to Edward who, as we have seen, had developed a perhaps rather excessive regard for money.

The Elgars' position at this time was rather an unfortunate one and was not eased by a view of what was due to them which necessitated Edward's always travelling first class and Alice's never keeping less than two maids. But, although it is thus absurd to pretend that they ever knew poverty as it was known to Mozart and Schubert, the fact remains that for many years Edward earned virtually nothing from the work by which he is known today.

'It does seem,' Alice said to me on one occasion, 'as if Edward never will earn any money by writing music.'

The shortage of money preyed sadly on his nerves and he never managed to achieve a philosophical attitude to it. I suppose it is fairly clear to anyone who knows the overture *Froissart* that he had a feeling for the colours and patterns of heraldry and on one occasion he confessed to wanting to paint heraldic designs, but complained that he could not afford the colours. I therefore bought a paint-box with gold and silver in little shells and offered it to him. To my surprise and sorrow, however, the gift, so far from pleasing him, hurt him bitterly by emphasizing —as he saw it—his poverty. It was useless to tell him that I had only bought the paints because I had chanced to have the money by me at the moment and had known what he wanted. All he could see was the gross unfairness of his not having the money for so trifling a purchase.

Another instance that comes to mind also ended rather unhappily. One night Dr Rapson, who was Professor of Sanskrit at Cambridge and keeper of Indian coins at the British Museum came to dinner at The Mount and I asked Edward to meet him. Professor Rapson was extremely polite to the younger man and succeeded in drawing him out and making him speak about his work with the result that they stayed till a late hour, talking over the firelight. At that time Edward was playing with the idea of a work based on Rabelais and Professor Rapson was delighted with his courage in breaking away from the tradition of 'all those dreary oratorios'.

Edward had a gold coin on his watch chain which glinted in the firelight and caught Professor Rapson's eye.

'May I make a shot?' he asked suddenly. 'That coin of yours looks like a gold mohur.'

Edward explained that his wife's father had brought it from India.

The Professor did not examine it but said casually that if it were genuine it would be very valuable.

Some days later Edward remembered the conversation and hopefully sent the coin to the British Museum for examination with a view to sale. Fate however was once more against him and another frustration in store. The mohur was a fake of no value and was not even of gold. The incident, trivial in itself, was one of many which helped to deepen in him the hopelessness of ever gaining money with the slightest ease.

If money were to be made, then, he must continue to earn it as other composers had done, and were doing, by teaching, performing or conducting. And here his increasing fame began to help him. It would have helped him more had he had any true gift in these directions but in reality he was a composer and little else. Of his teaching enough has perhaps been said. As a performer he suffered from a shyness which completely prevented his putting any warmth into his playing though it did not interfere with his excellence as an orchestral leader.

As an orchestral leader he was helped by the fact that he could lose his shyness in the ensemble, but by 1897 he was beginning to regard such work as beneath his dignity. There was one occasion at about this time when, walking with me in Worcester, he heard the orchestral rehearsals for the Festival and pricked up his ears like an old war-house at the hint of battle.

'Why don't you join them?' I asked.

The suggestion was not welcomed.

It was as a conductor therefore that he next tried to develop.

In those years in the country districts we depended for music mainly on the efforts of a few amateur organizations in various centres. In addition to a large number of instrumentalists in Malvern and Worcester there were such bodies as Edward's Ladies' Orchestral Class, our 'Big Orchy' at Malvern and a few quartet parties which practised privately, besides a large number of fairly competent singers who only needed banding into a choir.

Home music-making, which is now almost extinct, was then a flourishing interest. The Fittons' quartet party has already been mentioned and there were many others only slightly less accomplished. Even the less gifted showed an immense enthusiasm which only needed canalizing. Thus there was a Mr Dyke Acland who was manager of the local bank and to whom Edward dedicated his *Sursum Corda*. Mr Acland played the 'cello very industriously and was a great lover of the older classics. (He hated Wagner and believed that music had reached its highest expression in Mendelssohn.) Such was his enthusiasm that he was always willing to play anywhere for any cause and for any length of time with the result that Mrs Acland, a very competent pianist who was usually coerced into accompanying him, was sometimes ready to drop off the stool from sheer exhaustion.

In 1897 the happy idea occurred to someone of crystallizing all the talent of the district into one body under the direction of Edward Elgar. The scheme was welcomed almost at once. Worcester had never been slow to recognize his talents and with a little beating up, we managed to collect a very large number of subscribers. Not that everyone was as hopeful as we of success. Old Mrs Fitton pointed out from the start that Edward had not the precise qualities to hold such an organization together.

'He'll throw it up as soon as he gets tired of it,' she said.

But most of us were hopeful and enthusiastic.

The Worcestershire Philharmonic Society was not organized without some of the ill-feeling that seems to be inseparable from musical undertakings. There had existed in Worcester for many years a society which, under the leadership of a distinguished musician, had done valuable work. But the conductor was an ageing man, his programmes had become dull and conventional and a new influence was clearly needed. His club was too important to be absorbed into the new one and too nearly moribund to escape extinction in the resulting conflict of loyalties. Whether a greater tact on Edward's part might have averted the bitterness of that conflict is perhaps doubtful, but tact was certainly not exercised. The old conductor had the humiliation of seeing his followers trickle away to the Worcester Philharmonic Society and Edward was not very successful in concealing his satisfaction at having absorbed them.

The Philharmonic Society had from the outset the advantage of an influential backing. Recruitment to its ranks, vigorously undertaken by a few enthusiasts, was fairly easy since those who could play an instrument readily joined the orchestra, those who sang could be pressed into the choir and those who did neither swelled the audience and were glad of an excuse for driving into Worcester, lunching with friends and driving home again. Often there would be a party after the concert in one of the roomy eighteenth-century houses which had not then been turned into shops. It was at these that Herr Ettling made some of his most flamboyantly incongruous appearances.

On one occasion a number of friends were being entertained in this way in Foregate Street by a Worcester solicitor, Mr Hyde, whose daughter was a member of the Society. Herr Ettling felt that things needed enlivening and proceeded to do a few conjuring tricks, taking various small possessions from the guests and putting them in a hat. Suddenly Mr Hyde, who had been asked for someone's address, felt in his pocket and found that his wallet was missing.

'Ah,' he said 'another of Herr Ettling's little jokes!'

But Herr Ettling looked very embarrassed and said that he had not taken the pocket book.

An extremely uncomfortable scene followed. Everyone felt that Herr Ettling must be treated in a sporting way but that after all he was a foreigner. . . . Poor Edward, who had introduced this strange dissonance into the Hydes' domestic harmony, looked as if he would like to sink through the floor. Fortunately, however, Mr Hyde's tact saved the situation. Quietly dispatching one of his sons to the office, he was able himself to produce the wallet which had been left in his desk.

That the Worcestershire Philharmonic Society was lucky in having for its director so distinguished a musician as Edward is of course obvious. But it is equally true that the Society was of considerable value to him. In the first place it did something to counterbalance the deficiencies of his training as a musician. It must always be remembered in any study of his character and behaviour that his natural egotism had never had the valuable corrective of life in a big academy, with its discipline, friendly rivalry and good-natured criticism. Lacking this corrective he could not be blamed for developing into a rather intolerant and difficult artist unable to bear the faintest breath of criticism. Moreover marriage, which might have been expected to supply an element of criticism, failed in his case to do anything of the kind since Alice was too blinded by her admiration of him ever to notice defects which were glaringly obvious to everyone else. Had she been able to induce him to take criticism in an easy, good-humoured way he would have been spared much bitterness. Unfortunately, she also took a far too one-sided view of his critics.

In this connection, one reads with surprise a sentence by Mr Basil Maine, 'Shrewd judgement and knowledge of the human factor,' writes Mr Maine, 'qualifications, which many a conductor spends half his life in acquiring, were already Elgar's before he was thirty.' The book from which this quotation is taken was written during Edward's lifetime and may in consequence be taken by many as authoritative but one cannot help wondering where Mr Maine, who was not born when Edward

was thirty, obtained so astonishing a piece of information. The
fact is that by the time Edward was forty, and for long afterwards, he had no technique whatever for dealing with such a
body of people as we are now considering.

This deficiency however, the Worcestershire Philharmonic
Society did something to modify. It came too late in his life to
cure him, but some of his worst angularities it did rub off.
Somehow or other the disparate elements in the society had to
be welded into a whole, the public faced and a certain amount of
criticism endured. A more obvious gain to Edward was that the
Society provided him with an instrument for experiments in
part-writing and orchestration. It may of course be argued that
by 1897 he had acquired such a mastery of both as to be in no
need of any such instrument but throughout the years of his
association with the Society he was constantly writing little
experimental counterpoints—sometimes for addition to standard works, sometimes for his own—which we were asked to
play in order that he might test the actual sound of vocal or
instrumental effects which he had devised but had only heard
in imagination. The instrument may not have been first-rate
but with an orchestra of about fifty—which for public performances was stiffened by the addition of professionals—and
a choir of a hundred voices, it was not negligible.

Yet a further advantage arose from Edward's enthusiasm for
what was newest and most advanced in the music of the time.
From the start he had ambitions for the Society far beyond
those of the ordinary provincial music-club of that time and an
examination of the programmes shows that the works chosen
were anything but conventional. The first concert included a
little-known cantata by Humperdinck (which was given twice
in the one programme) and at subsequent concerts we sang or
played new works by Mackenzie, Bantock, Stanford, Parry,
Walford Davies and Philipp Wolframm. Some of these composers had similar organizations of their own and, while it
would be unjust to say that Edward chose the works of com-

posers able to reciprocate by performing works of his, some of them did in fact do so to his advantage.

We started with immense enthusiasm. Edward had been given a completely free hand in the choice of the programme and, although he had selected Humperdinck's *Die Wahlfahrt nach Kevlaar* for the first concert, and insisted on doing it in German, a language of which ninety-nine per cent of the choir knew nothing, the practices were well-attended and the work attacked with good-humoured determination. That the result was more satisfactory musically than linguistically is not surprising when one remembers that the conductor knew little more German than his choir. Alice of course spoke it fluently as did Miss Norbury, one of the secretaries, but for the most part strange chewing noises were produced that sounded like no known European language. Nevertheless a success was made with the local public.

Between 1898 and 1903 Edward conducted twelve programmes, three additional ones being contributed by the Brodsky Quartet. That he did not conduct more was due to a disagreement which, starting almost at the outset, gradually became more and more bitter until it ended in a quarrel that could not be healed.

In order to understand the cause of this disagreement it is necessary to remember that there was in his character a bitterness which, whatever its original cause, found expression in a hatred for those more fortunately placed than himself, but which, with the perversity of human nature, did not prevent him from trying to identify himself with them. As director of the Worcestershire Philharmonic Society he found himself at last in command of a group of the very class of people whose social superiority had hurt him and the situation was one of which he could hardly help taking advantage. It is not suggested that he deliberately revenged himself on the members but rather that their easy manners, by emphasizing in contrast the clumsiness of his own, irritated him into extreme impatience with

purely musical failings. Things were undoubtedly difficult for
him. He felt that he deserved something much better than the
members could give him, especially when in cold weather the
drive into Worcester had numbed the players' fingers and the
rehearsals were in an unheated room. But it is also true that,
being anything but a born teacher, he could not make the best
of the talent that was available. His wide vague beat would
sometimes baffle the best of us and in matters of interpretation
he seemed incapable of explaining exactly what he wanted.
Again and again he would stand shading his eyes with one hand
(a very characteristic position) and would exclaim angrily 'No,
no, that was all wrong', until the more sensitive were nearly in
tears and the more stolid were reduced to a mulish obstinacy.

On one occasion Miss Norbury was attempting a difficult
piano accompaniment over which she made one or two stumbles.
White with rage, Edward suddenly shouted at me, 'Here! You
do it!'

It was noticeable, moreover, that his contempt was spread
so as to include the audiences. In a programme note to Philipp
Wolframm's *Ein Weihnachts Mysterium* he wrote:

'The members of the Philharmonic Society will not treat the
performance as an ordinary conventional concert, which in
England is supposed to begin "loud" and end "louder" whereupon the audience is dismissed with a feeling of satisfaction that
they have not met altogether in vain. . . .'

The precise cause of the ultimate break has never been known
but it was obvious by the sixteenth concert that his patience was
fast giving out. It may have been, as was suggested by some,
that he wanted a higher fee but yet did not like to ask for it, or
that he was getting desperate over his own failure to handle his
forces. English musical societies are used to being cursed by
their conductors and the Worcestershire Philharmonic took its
castigations as others have done, with philosophy. It had indeed
given him everything in its powers. It had followed him in a
choice of programmes which often contained works that were

by no means obvious box-office attractions (for example Berlioz's *Enfance du Christ* and his own *The Dream of Gerontius* known at that time only for its failure at the Birmingham Triennial Festival of 1900). It had engaged the best artists and had gladly fallen in with his stipulation that all the instruments specified by a composer must be included at whatever cost. What it could not do and what he was incapable of teaching it to do was to be an instrument worthy of the music performed.

Rehearsals for Wilhelm Berger's *Der Totentanz* had gone particularly badly. The programme, which contained also a work by Hugo Wolf and Berlioz's Romeo and Juliet symphony, was exacting no doubt for the conductor as well as the members, and by the last practice everyone's nerves had become frayed. The playing became rougher and rougher, the singing more and more inaccurate until suddenly Edward flung down the stick, announced that he would not conduct the concert and stormed out of the room.

There was a moment's stupefaction followed by loudly expressed resentment. It was all very well, the members felt, for him to have chosen a programme beyond their powers to perform and for him then to refuse to conduct it. But the solo singers and extra instrumentalists had been engaged, a hall hired and many other expenses involved which had somehow to be met.

A committee meeting was hurriedly called at which it was decided, since Edward appeared to mean what he had said, to ask Granville Bantock to conduct the concert instead. But Dr Bantock, who was obviously puzzled, naturally refused to take over the direction in such circumstances and a further meeting had to be arranged between Edward, Bantock and representatives of the Society. At this meeting Edward's attitude was vague, confused and difficult to understand. Various offers were made but it seemed as if, having played his trump card, he refused to take the trick or indeed to say what he really wished. Ultimately it was agreed that Bantock should direct the concert and that Edward should become a vice-president of the Society.

Had he expected his refusal to conduct the concert to be taken seriously? Would he have returned for a higher fee? We shall never know. A subsequent meeting was held to persuade him to reconsider his resignation and a minority did in fact suggest a larger fee. But no reconciliation was really effected, ill-feeling was general and Granville Bantock succeeded him in Worcester as was later to happen in Birmingham.

W. H. Reed's description of this incident is a masterpiece of understatement:

'Such was the pressure of work and the strain of his numerous engagements upon Elgar at this time,' he says, 'that he had reluctantly to resign his conductorship of the Worcester Philharmonic Society.'

13

Caractacus

The story of Edward's association with the Worcestershire Philharmonic Society, having been told in continuous form, has taken us far beyond the point reached in the main narrative, to which we now return.

The production of *King Olaf* was followed by a fallow period which, although no doubt inevitable, was rather an anxiety to those of us who were hoping to see Edward write the great work of which increasingly we believed him to be capable. Mr Nettel has given a fine account of the effect made by *Olaf's* freshness and originality, not only at its first performance, but even on those who heard mere snatches of its rehearsals. While far in advance of anything else of the kind being turned out by English composers of that time, however, it could hardly be considered wholly successful and the question arose whether Edward could write a work as superior to *Olaf* as *Olaf* had been to, say, *The Black Knight*. It was nearly three years before this question was answered.

In the meantime there had been a change of some importance in Edward's conditions of work. For some time he had been rather tired of 'Forli' and had begun to think of moving farther away from what was becoming a built-up district. When therefore the squire of Birchwood, a Mr Little, offered him the use of a cottage on the estate he gladly accepted. This cottage was too small to serve as a permanent home but it made a delightful woodland retreat to which he could retire when he needed peace from domestic worries.

Birchwood is a hamlet about half a mile to the right of the old Worcester–Hereford road between Leigh Sinton and Storridge and it had in those days a charm which has now largely vanished. Visitors who make the pilgrimage to Birchwood Lodge today are in fact often puzzled to understand what Edward could have seen in it, for the wood has been cut down and the cottage, at best an ugly Noah's ark of a place covered with stucco and surrounded with spiked railings, has been enlarged and resounds to the clatter of milk churns. All that remains of the old beauty indeed is a plantation on the hillside and the view over Birchwood Common. But in 1898 the cottage stood just inside the entrance to a thick and mysterious wood through which one could wander downhill to the valley.

Sir Arnold Bax, who was taken there in 1901 by George Aldar, the horn player, has truly said that Birchwood was one of the most important influences in Elgar's life. He went there in the first place mainly as an escape, but as time went on he became deeply affected by the peace of the woods and the sounds that floated in through the windows. In the end he left it—as he was often to leave other homes—through a habitual restlessness, but in later life he always remembered Birchwood with the deepest affection.

I believe I was the first of his friends to be taken to the cottage for it was not furnished when I went and he told me how he intended to use its small rooms. His study—as at nearly all the other houses he took—was to be on the first floor as soon as a piano could be sent over from Worcester, the downstairs rooms being used as living-room and kitchen. Here, he felt, was at last the peace in which he could write.

A number of schemes conceived at Birchwood never came to fruition. There was to have been, for instance, an opera suggested by his new surroundings and based on Hewlett's *The Forest Lovers*, but he was unable or unwilling to work with the lady who held the dramatic rights and the plan fizzled out. In view of the opinion expressed by some critics that he had not the ability required in opera to crystallize a situation into a few notes it is unfortunate that neither *The Forest Lovers* nor *The Spanish Lady*, on which he was engaged when he died, was completed. Three very important works did however emerge from this period.

The success of *King Olaf* had led, amongst much else, to a commission for a new choral work from the committee of the Leeds Festival and this Edward fulfilled with a cantata based on the subject of Caractacus and his last stand against the Romans. The new work, the libretto of which was supplied by Mr H. A. Acworth, was begun early in the year 1898 and rapidly completed in the solitude of the cottage. Edward was undoubtedly fired by the legend that the actual battle had taken place at the British Camp in the Malvern Hills, not far from where he was actually writing, and he worked relatively easily and with great enthusiasm. The first performance was given at Leeds on 5 October.

I was fortunate enough to be present for the occasion. The Lord Mayor of Leeds, Mr C. F. Tetley, whose two daughters were at The Mount, asked me to stay with his family for the week. This was a pleasant experience as the Tetleys, who have remained my friends to this day, were exceedingly kind and I was glad of a chance to compare a big North Country festival with those of the Three Choirs.

The difference was, as it turned out, very marked. The Leeds Festival was a secular meeting, the first of a series having been arranged in connection with the opening of the Town Hall by Queen Victoria, and the first thing that struck me in consequence was that the audience were a good deal less clerical, less County and a good deal more fashionable and opulent than those in my own district. The very programme was lavish for, in addition to Edward's cantata, there were works by Humperdinck, Stanford, Alan Gray, Cowen and Otto Goldschmidt.

Musically the festival was distinguished by the fine choral singing for which Yorkshire is noted and by a certain rather business-like efficiency. Sullivan, next to whom I was placed at lunch one morning, was conductor-in-chief for the last time that year. He was already a doomed man and had to direct the performances from a chair.

For Edward the occasion was one of great anxiety as the Leeds Festival was immensely more important than that of Hanley. Moreover, though *King Olaf* had marked him as a composer of great promise, he was as yet by no means regarded as the peer of Cowen, Stanford or Sullivan, who were established favourites. We were thus all on tenterhooks to hear how the cantata would fare. I had heard a good many scraps played but could not quite feel that they would build up into a satisfactory whole and I could hardly wait for the performance. But at last its turn came, the soloists (Medore Henson, Edward Lloyd, Andrew Black, John Browning and Charles Knowles) and the magnificent choir sang it for all it was worth despite Edward's rather uncertain direction. The applause was loud and prolonged . . . and yet I was a little doubtful.

Caractacus, without exactly failing to maintain Edward's reputation, had done little to increase it. The main trouble—of especial interest having regard to his operatic ambitions—is that a dramatic story receives essentially non-dramatic treatment, but there are many other flaws. Thus the feeble libretto is often a hindrance, making the marriage of words and music an unhappy union and, although there are fine passages, so far from building up into a satisfactory whole, they remain isolated patches. Mr Dunhill sees in the music 'evidence of an advance, technically, on Elgar's previous choral writing', but regards it as a great disappointment, coming after *King Olaf*. 'What', he asks 'can a serious composer be expected to do with such stuff as this ?—

'My heart is bright as morning light,
And tender as the flower,

> For here I rove to meet my love
> In this, the chosen hour.'

The closing chorus in which the Romans, having beaten the British, sing (in Rome) of a day to come when "the nations all shall stand, And hymn the praise of Britain, Like brothers hand in hand" is so wildly absurd as seriously to endanger the whole cantata. Certainly Mr Acworth beat even Longfellow here.

The work was dedicated by permission to Queen Victoria.

Edward, who never enjoyed any festival of his earlier years, was particularly unhappy at this one. Nervous and never too sure of himself, he needed an immense amount of encouragement before he was at anything like his best and, while in Worcester, where by now he had become something of a lion, this stimulus was always forthcoming, it was a different matter at Leeds which had known and entertained most of the greater composers of the later Nineteenth Century. Here he was merely one of a group and by no means the most important member of it, with the result that although the committee treated him with courtesy—and such committees consisted of very cultured people—he felt insulted and hurt.

The fact is of course that this was one more example of the absurd injustice which necessitates a composer's attempting to be a performer. The Leeds committee found Edward ill-tempered and difficult but it may be that they did not realize the state of his mind. After the nervous strain of creating one of his major works he was in no mood to supervise the details of its performance, still less to listen to the chatter of either admirers or detractors.

When it was all over he rushed back to Malvern with the air of one who has fought, and is inclined to think he has lost—a heavy engagement.

14

The Variations 1898-9

Whatever may have been the success of *Caractacus*—and for all its unevenness this cantata gained a hold it has subsequently never quite lost—it did nothing to prepare Edward's friends for the sudden leap into fame which he made with the work which followed it.

One autumn afternoon, shortly after the Leeds Festival, he came to The Mount in the rather excited state which usually indicated some new inspiration and played me a sixteen-bar tune on the piano. I thought it wistful but hardly of outstanding interest and asked what it was. So far as I remember he did not answer the question but continued to play, apparently extemporizing, a set of variations each of which, he said, represented a friend. The first, which added a graceful triplet figure to an altered version of the theme was his wife, the second (much more effective on the piano than in the subsequent orchestral version) poked fun at the toccata-like figure with which his friend H. D. Steuart-Powell warmed up his hands before playing.

In the weeks that followed I heard much of the sad little tune and of the variations which were being grown from it. The supposed enigmatical significance was not, I think, mentioned at that time though much was made of it later on. Towards the end of his life Edward said that the Enigma tune expressed his feeling of loneliness as an artist and, unlike many such interpretations, this one seems sufficiently accurate.

At the time, he was far more concerned with the variations than with the underlying theme and constantly challenged me to guess whom they represented. But by 1898 the Elgars had acquaintances in a number of detached circles and it is probably true that practically none of the variation subjects can have known all the others. Moreover those I did know seemed often to have been dressed in unwontedly brilliant clothes. Thus Jaeger, a true friend but an almost commonplace little German, seemed, despite the obvious pun, rather strangely cast for the part of Nimrod and the music of his variation, though not marked *nobilmente*, for once, emphasizes nobility rather than any other quality, and in fact begins with a manifest reference to the second movement of Beethoven's sonata, op. 13. In many cases, however, the portraiture was astonishingly accurate and the translation of physical or mental characteristics into musical terms wonderfully ingenious. As the work progressed, indeed, and variation was added to variation, I realized that the complete set, when illuminated by Edward's brilliant orchestration, might show an enormous advance on anything he had previously written.

The circumstances of the first performance, which took place on 19 June, 1899 at a Richter concert in the old St James's Hall, illustrate a number of Edward's oddest traits of character. By this time he had really come to believe, as Mr Nettel points out in *Ordeal by Music*, that there was a secret conspiracy to boycott his work in London. When, however, he wrote to Miss Penny that Richter would play the Variations in the summer—'if he is not prevented by certain London —— (mystery)' he was surely thinking, not as Mr Nettel suggests, of the critics so much as of those musicians whom he used to call the 'academics' and for whom, through envy of their established position, he had conceived an unreasonable dislike and distrust.

On this occasion, the distrust was particularly unjustifiable for, although he allowed his Malvern friends to suppose that the merit of the Variations had appealed to Richter despite the

opposition of London's academic musicians, we have it on the
authority of Dr Vaughan Williams that, 'it was Hubert Parry,
who, when he saw the manuscript score, left his after-dinner
armchair and rushed out into the rain to show it to Richter.'
There is also evidence that both Stanford and Sir Alexander
Mackenzie went out of their way to give help and encouragement.

Whatever the route by which the work reached Richter, there
was no doubt of his enthusiasm for it or of the immense value
of the send-off which first performance by him gave it. There
has in recent years been a tendency—shown especially by Sir
Thomas Beecham and Ernest Newman—to reassess Richter's
value, and it must be admitted that a conductor who could
calmly dismiss French music as non-existent not only had serious
limitations but was likely to add to those unsatisfactory influences on Elgar of which Jaeger's was perhaps then the chief.
But in 1899 Richter's power was so enormous that to be taken
up by him assured a measure of recognition that could be obtained in no other way.

The first performance, unlike those of many of Edward's
other works, was an immense success. The opening theme,
which had seemed a little thin and ineffective on the piano, took
on a wholly Elgarian poignancy when played by strings and, as
the changing moods of the variations succeeded one another,
tender, gay, and playful in turn many of the audience felt profoundly moved. It was not merely that Edward had beyond all
doubt written the masterpiece for which his friends had been
waiting. In it he had expressed a depth of affection for them
which some had hardly suspected him of feeling and which he
could have conveyed in no other way.

Since it was the programme note of that concert which contained the only information that Edward ever gave regarding
the enigmatic factor in the variations we shall quote the relevant
passage:

'On being asked for some elucidation of "the composer's

intentions" Mr. Edgar [*sic*] replied, "'It is true that I have
sketched for their amusement and mine the idosyncracies of
fourteen of my friends, not necessarily musicians, but this is a
personal matter and need not have been mentioned publicly. . . .
The Enigma I will not explain—its 'dark saying' must be left
unguessed and I warn you that the apparent connection between
the Variations and the Theme is often of the slightest nature;
further through and over the whole set another and larger
theme 'goes' but is not played. . . . So the principal theme
never appears, even as in some late dramas—*e.g.* Maeterlinck's
L'Intruse and *Les Sept Princesses*—the chief character is never
on the stage.'"

Exactly what this meant no one has ever known and Edward
never explained or amplified it. The obvious inference is that
Enigma (the name of the theme on which the variations are
based) is not so much an original piece of music in its own right
as a counterpoint built to fit some well known tune, and an
immense amount of patience has been expended on finding the
tune in question. The difficulties that arise however are surprisingly great. Thus, although *Enigma*, like countless other tunes,
is sixteen bars long, the disposition of those bars is very unusual.
Most tunes of this length consist of an eight-bar sentence which is
repeated with a different cadence, but *Enigma* is based on a scheme
of six plus four plus six. That is to say that a six-bar sentence
in G minor is followed by a four-bar sentence in G major after
which the original six bars in G minor are repeated. To find a
solution therefore one would first have to discover another
tune based on the same bizarre scheme. As it is, the numberless
tunes which fit the length of *Enigma* fail altogether to match its
content. No one has even found another tune that would fit its
bass, which as Tovey pointed out in dismissing Mr Richard
Powell's ingenious *Auld Lang Syne* solution, Elgar would certainly have demanded.

But even supposing that a tune were found that fitted *Enigma*,
it would not fulfil the conditions of the programme-note since

no theme ever conceived—no musical theme at least—could 'go' with the whole set of variations, which vary in length, and of which two (the *Intermezzo* and *Romanza*) bear only the most distant relationship to *Enigma*.

This led Ernest Newman to suggest that the theme which 'goes' through and over the whole set is the non-musical one of friendship, and this, on the whole seems to be the most satisfactory solution. And yet . . . *Enigma* with its persistent off-beat accents and its interrupted melodic line does strike those who hear it for the first time as an accompaniment rather than a tune. And the programme-note mentions a 'theme which is not played' seeming to imply that it could be played. Moreover we are told that it never appears; yet if the theme is friendship, it does appear as far as is humanly possible. The puzzle must therefore be regarded as unsolved and seems likely to remain so. It may be added that Edward rejected every musical solution of the puzzle offered him.

'The probability is,' wrote W. H. Reed, 'that his friend A. J. Jaeger was right when he told an inquirer that it was "a bit of Elgar's humour".' The writer of this volume [*i.e.* W. H. Reed] although one of Elgar's closest friends for nearly thirty years, did not venture to ask him the meaning until very nearly the end of his life, and he feels quite sure that he would have told him then if it was really based on another tune. He only said, with the well-known twinkle in his eye: 'Ah, that's telling!' It was indeed as far as the present writer is concerned for it told that Jaeger was right, as he had in fact long suspected, knowing the little twist in Elgar's mind about such things and the keen enjoyment he derived from puzzling people.

'He was himself the Enigma, and remained so to the end of his life.'

Mrs Richard Powell ('Dorabella'), on the other hand, while rejecting her husband's *Auld Lang Syne* argument believes that a musical solution exists and that 'when it has been found, there will be no room for any doubt that it is the right one'.

Whatever the solution of the Enigma might be Edward knew that his scheme of dedicating each variation to a friend, whose (mostly) non-musical characteristics it depicted, was not wholly original. Schumann had done something of the kind in *Carnival* and Tchaikovski had actually written what Gerald Abraham calls a set of 'enigma variations' in his *Trio in Memory of a Great Artist* (Nicolas Rubinstein). Here not only had the theme a private association but each variation referred to some detail of Rubinsteins career in a way to which no key has ever been found.

In Elgar's work, however, it is only the theme that puzzles us. In the case of all but one of the variations the identity of the subjects has long been discovered. What does not seem to be generally known is that two further variations, dedicated respectively to Parry and Sullivan, were discarded. The difficulty with these was that as Edward did not really know either of the two composers well he could only represent them by a pastiche of their styles whereas the aim of the variations was to portray non-musical characteristics in music.

It has often been said that an acquaintance with the personalities of the friends concerned makes no difference to one's appreciation of the variations as music, and indeed Edward—having evidently mentioned it—said that the matter need never have been mentioned. But, since the aim of the present study is biographical rather than musical and since these people did undoubtedly inspire the variations that bear their initials or nicknames, a sketch of them may not be thought out of place. It may be added that if conductors always remembered the pictorial significance of some of the numbers (for instance 'W.N.', in which there is a musical interpretation of a woman's laugh, which in performance too often sounds stiff and pointless) we might be brought a good deal nearer to Edward's musical intentions.

He himself wrote a set of notes on the variation subjects for the Aeolian Company's pianola rolls and these notes, illustrated

by a facsimile of the first page of the score of each variation and
a reproduction of a contemporary photograph of its subject,
taken from Mrs Elgar Blake's Enigma Variations panel at
Broadheath, have been published by Novello in a pleasant little
pamphlet called *My Friends Pictured Within*. These notes, though
written a quarter of a century after the variations, must of
course, be taken as authoritative but they differ in some details
from what he told me in 1898 and in one case in even the identity of the person concerned. As moreover the notes are extremely reticent regarding the personalities of some of the sitters
it may be as well to amplify the information given from my own
memories of Edward's conversation.

No. 1 (C.A.E.) is of course Alice, his wife. This variation is
really, as Edward said in his notes 'a prolongation of the theme
with what I wished to be romantic and delicate additions; those
who knew C.A.E. will understand this reference to one whose
life was a romantic and delicate inspiration.' And indeed no
more graceful tribute could have been paid to the woman who
had devoted her whole life to his happiness.

No. 2 (H.D.S.-P.) refers, to Hew David Steuart-Powell with
whom Edward (violin) and Basil Nevinson ('cello; see Variation 12) used to play pianoforte trios. It can hardly be said that
a non-musical characteristic is illustrated here or that the result
sounds like a toccata. In his notes Edward said he had humor-
ously travestied his friend's characteristic diatonic run over the
keys before beginning to play, and admitted that the effect was
chromatic beyond H.D.S.-P.'s liking. Actually it sounds rather
like Richard Strauss's musical illustration of carping critics.

No. 3 (R.B.T.) is a portrait of Richard Baxter Townshend.
Mr Townsend was the author of the 'Tenderfoot' books and
something of an oddity; he looks indeed in the portrait at Broadheath as much like a woman as a man. His voice had never
really broken and was very high-pitched. By some irony he was
cast in an amateur play for the part of a gruff old man but, although he did his best, could not keep his voice down to the

required pitch and occasionally produced some absurd high notes. The prominence of oboe and bassoons in the variation refers to this incident.

No. 4 (W.M.B.) is equally successful. W. Meath Baker of Hasfield Court was R.B.T.'s brother-in-law, the latter having married one of W.M.B.'s sisters. (Another sister married the Rev. Alfred Penny of Wolverhampton whose daughter by a previous marriage was the subject of Variation No. 10, *Dorabella*). The portrait is of a bluff genial character who in leaving the room accidentally slams the door.

No. 5 (R.P.A.) deals with R. P. Arnold a son of Matthew Arnold and thus a cousin of Mrs Humphrey Ward and of her nephews Julian and Aldous Huxley. His pleasant, scholarly character is conveyed very successfully.

No. 6 (Ysobel) is Isabel Fitton of Malvern. (The fussy perversion of her name is pure Elgar.) It is difficult for me to write of her with detachment even today several years after her death for she was one of my dearest friends and I still feel her loss. She was tall, ardent, witty and extremely musical and she was endeared to me by invariably seeing the same jokes. The variation is a tribute to her unselfish enterprise in learning the viola which was needed to help our local music-making. 'The opening bar, a phrase made use of throughout the variation,' says Edward in his notes, 'is an exercise for crossing the strings—a difficulty for beginners.'

No. 7 (Troyte) is of course A. Troyte Griffith—nicknamed 'The Ninepin'. I always understood that this variation was intended to suggest skittles being bowled over. W. H. Reed was told that the cross-rhythm beaten out by the drums represented Troyte's habit of saying the unexpected, but Edward writes quite a 'programme' in which maladroit efforts by the subject to play the piano are corrected by the composer who gives a final 'slam' to the variation.

No. 8 (W.N.) is a portrait of Winifred Norbury one of the secretaries of the Worcestershire Philharmonic Society and a devoted friend of the Elgars. In his notes Edward said that the variation was in reality suggested by an eighteenth-century house (presumably Sherridge) but that as W.N. was more connected with music than the rest of her family, her initials headed the movement. Nevertheless, it was unmistakably her laugh that was denoted by the arching little arpeggio figure.

No. 9 (Nimrod) is the most famous of all the variations and is dedicated to, rather than depicts, August Jaeger. Edward himself seemed to feel a certain incongruity in the dedication and explained that 'something ardent and mercurial in addition to the slow movement would have been needed to portray the character and temperament of A. J. Jaeger'. This is a judgement with which not all would concur.

This ninth variation has in recent years become the standard elegy for musicians and indeed its palpably elegiac quality was made fitting by Jaeger's tragically early death. The tune is a noble one but is running the risk of too great a popularity.

No. 10 (*Dorabella*; Intermezzo) is hardly a variation on the Enigma theme at all. In his notes on the variation subjects Edward was oddly reticent about the women and even as we shall see changed his mind as to the identity of one of them. Miss Dora Penny, the third member of the Hasfield Court group to be included, was a frequent visitor to 'Forli' and later to the Elgars' other houses to which, when the bicycle became popular, she would often ride over from Wolverhampton. She herself has told in her book of this variation's connection with her solo dancing but does not mention that it reproduces also the rhythm of her speech. The title of course comes from Mozart's *Cosi Fan Tutte*.

No. 11 (G.R.S.) is the most successfully illustrative of all the variations. Dr George Robertson Sinclair was for twenty-seven years the organist of Hereford Cathedral where he exerted a very good influence on the music. The hero of the eleventh variation however, is really Dan, Dr Sinclair's bulldog. One afternoon when Edward was visiting Dr Sinclair they took Dan for a walk by the Wye. He was a clumsy animal and, missing his foot-ing, rolled down the bank into the river with a tremendous splash. Dr Sinclair challenged Edward to put the incident to music, which he did. The splash, the paddling and even the 'rejoicing bark on landing' are all faithfully reproduced.

No. 12 (B.G.N.) is Basil G. Nevinson the 'cellist of the Elgar-Steuart-Powell, Nevinson trio. He was a London friend of whose hospitality Edward often availed himself when he had to go up to town.

No. 13 (xxx 'Romanza') is in itself something of an enigma. For many years no name was publicly mentioned in connection with this variation which, like No. 10, is practically unrelated to the theme. But Edward told me quite clearly and unequivo-cally whom it represented and I always supposed that his reason for withholding this lady's name was that extremely intimate and personal feelings were concerned. The throbbing and the quotation from *Calm Sea and Prosperous Voyage* (which might almost equally well come from the Schumann pianoforte con-certo or *Leonora No. 3*) bore no reference to the liner and the sea voyage which were afterwards associated with this variation but, as might be expected in a movement named 'Romanza', expressed something very different.

The present dedication to Lady Mary Lygon (later Trefusis) was really the result of a false inference which Edward rather surprisingly allowed. It was of course some time before the variations achieved a very wide popularity or the identity of the subjects became a matter of much interest. The owners of the initials and nicknames were quickly recognized but at first no one bothered about the three stars. As the work increased in fame however their strange anonymity began to draw a certain amount of attention. And indeed Edward could hardly complain if, having been baffled by the secret of the Enigma theme, his friends turned rather eagerly to the solution of this less abstruse puzzle.

The internal evidence offered by this variation is rather vague.

Essentially romantic in feeling, it does (though, as I think, accidentally) suggest a seascape, the impression being deepened by the Mendelssohn quotation, the throb of the drums and the fact that a very similar effect is produced in one of the *Sea Pictures*. The conclusion was thus drawn that the lady, whoever she was, was on a voyage when the variation was written, and indeed Edward seems to have admitted, when pressed by inquirers for her identity, that she had been 'at sea'.

Someone then remembered that Lady Mary Lygon of Madresfield Court, near Malvern, had in fact visited her brother, who was Governor of New South Wales, at this time and she was henceforth assumed to be the subject of the movement.

It does not seem to have occurred to anyone that so persistent a lover of enigmas as Edward might have used the phrase 'at sea' in a figurative sense. But what really might have struck the inquirers was that, since the Variations were written by the end of 1898—they were scored for orchestra according to the autograph by 19 February 1899—and Lord Beauchamp did not become Governor until 1899, it was impossible that Lady Mary should have visited him in Australia till after the Romanza was actually on paper. I myself heard it before the end of 1898 and I think that Lady Mary sailed in the April or May of 1899.

At the time when Lady Mary's name was becoming attached to the Romanza I asked him why he did not deny the story. His reply was characteristic.

'What does it matter?' he said. That it might matter to the lady who had really formed the subject never, I am convinced, entered his head. Lady Mary, a very charming woman and a distinguished social figure, may have lent the work a certain cachet, fully justified, but the compliment has been more than returned since she is now chiefly remembered for her supposed connection with the Romanza. And there the matter ended. He clearly did not wish the true subject's name revealed (and, in his notes on the variations, actually mentioned Lady Mary and her voyage). I shall therefore follow the lead of Ernest Newman who is understood to have possessed certain confidential information which he refused to publish regarding the dedication of the Violin Concerto, and let her remain anonymous.

It may be mentioned that, when a selection of the Variations was made for the Elgar Memorial Service in Worcester Cathedral, only Nos. 1 (C.A.E.), 9 (Nimrod) and 13 (xxx) were played.

No. 14 (E.D.U.) is Edward's portrait of himself, the initials representing Alice's own nickname for him (Eddu). Since of course any piece of music by Edward would be in a musical sense something of a self-portrait E.D.U. may be considered a success but it does not indicate more than a fraction of his true character. The facet chosen here is that which gloried in pageantry though the influence of C.A.E. and Nimrod is gracefully acknowledged. This movement, which serves as a finale, gave Edward a good deal of trouble and there seems to have been some misconception as to how it reached its ultimate form. 'A report is now current,' wrote Sir Donald Tovey, 'that Elgar originally ended the Variations quietly and that this finale was forced upon him by more experienced friends. If this is true, for heaven's sake let every effort be made to recover the original finale.'

What actually happened was that the finale was found to be ineffective at the first performance and that Jaeger suggested that it should be lengthened. Jaeger was very liberal with criticisms of this kind and they were not always welcomed ('I will alter no more of *Caractacus*, short of burning the whole thing', Edward had written in 1898). In regard to the Enigma finale however, the suggestion was obviously wise and Edward's only problem was to know how to implement it. The difficulties are clearly set out in a letter to Jaeger published in Mr Basil Maine's book. 'Now look here, the movement was meant to be concise. Here's the difficulty of lengthening it. I could go on with those themes for half a day but the key G is exhausted.

The principal motive (Enigma) comes in grandioso on p. 35 in the tonic and it wouldn't do to bring it in again. Had I intended to make an extended movement this would have been in some related key, reserving the tonic for the final smash.' And later in the letter he adds, 'If I find after New Brighton that the end does not satisfy me I may recast the whole of the last movement but it's not possible to lengthen it with any satisfaction I fear. If I can find time to make a readable copy of my "end", I'll send it to you and you'll see how good E. Elgar is at heart.'

He managed to do so and a little later was able to write 'My dear J., You're a trump, I'm heartily glad you like the TAIL *I do* now its done. I haven't time for a word, only here's the M.S.'

The original finale, so far from needing to be recovered, was published in the piano score of the Variations. It may be said to use the same ideas less effectively. The ultimate orchestral version has been adversely criticized for its rather self-conscious air of pomp and circumstance and its addition of an organ to the already considerable volume of sound at the close. Those however, who can hear it unirritated by these considerations may feel with W. H. Reed that its exhilaration 'seems to convey that the subject of this virile and dominating music knew by some sort of intuition that this grand work would bring him recognition in the musical world at last'.

I believe it is true to say that Edward enjoyed the writing of the Variations more than that of any other work. At any rate he seemed happier to me. The fact is that for once he was not writing on commission but for the pleasure of doing so. I doubt indeed if he foresaw at the beginning that he had begun an important work. The thing started as a musical joke which ended almost fortuitously as one of his greatest masterpieces. One may add that, more than any of his other works, the Variations bring to mind the peculiar quality of the countryside in which they were conceived. The Malverns have a peculiarly welcoming kindliness about them which seems reflected in this music and so strong is the identification that even today half a century since Edward first played me the strangely wistful theme I cannot see the hills without seeming to hear it and without half expecting that at the next corner I shall meet him brandishing the manuscript of yet another variation.

15

Sea Pictures

There is no doubt that the production by Richter of the *Enigma Variations* in London in 1899 marked the biggest step forward that Edward had yet made. There were many signs that year of increasing recognition. Granville Bantock, who conducted the orchestra at New Brighton, gave an all-Elgar concert which included the *Variations*; *Sea Pictures*, a new song cycle was sung for the first time by Clara Butt at the Norwich Festival; Edward made an appearance at Covent Garden conducting his *Sword Song* from *Caractacus*, and *Scenes from the Bavarian Highlands*; *King Olaf* was given with immense success at Sheffield and *Caractacus* repeated at Leeds. And on 18 October he stayed with Sir Walter Parratt at Windsor when ten of his works were heard in the private chapel there, a Command Performance of *Sea Pictures* being given two days later. More important still, however, was the fact that, through Jaeger's influence, a German conductor, Dr Julius Buths, examined the *Variations*, realized their quality, and ultimately introduced them to the far larger public of his own country.

The effect of all this success on Edward was twofold. On the one hand he was pleased and became a little more important in his manner; but on the other he was inclined to be resentful that it had been delayed till he was forty-two. The resentment lasted till the end of his life and poisoned much of the happiness he might otherwise have felt. It never seems to have occurred to him that he could not reasonably expect success until he had written a really first-rate work, or that when he did so (in the *Variations*) recognition came astonishingly quickly. This resentment lured him into more than one foolish remark, some of which found their way into print. Thus in his own notes on the Variations, written about a quarter of a century later, he could speak of 'E.D.U.' as having been composed 'at a time when friends were dubious and generally discouraging as to the composer's musical future'. Actually there never was a time after, at any rate, 1892 when his friends were less than optimistic and encouraging. It was Edward himself who doubted, not they.

That he had a good deal to put up with is true. His success was still one of esteem rather than of money and there were many other irritations, not the least of which arose in connection with the Madresfield Competitions. Malvern, like other provincial centres, had followed the lead of Miss Wakefield at Kendal and in 1897 had started a music festival which was named after the seat of the Lygon family near by. By some stupid oversight on the part of the promoters, Edward, who as the leading musician of the district should have been consulted, was completely ignored. It was long before he forgave this slight. Then again the fame which was soon won by the *Variations* cast a certain reflected glory on the subjects, some of whom exasperated him by the airs they began to assume in consequence. I remember that at a party at the Hydes' shortly after the Variations had been produced and the initialled headings were still being discussed, one of the 'variants' came to me and said, 'Well, Miss Burley, I'm a variation. Are you?'

'No,' I answered gravely. 'I'm not a variation; I'm the theme.' Edward was much amused when I told him of this.

If the Elgars' financial position was not all they could have wished, however, it must have been easier by 1899 for in the March of that year they left 'Forli' and moved to a larger house. The new home, an altogether more modern place than the old, stood (and indeed stands) on the delightful road which skirts

the east side of the hills and runs from Great Malvern to Malvern Wells. To the left the ground falls away to the Severn
valley with Bredon Hill in the distance; to the right the well-
wooded lower slope of the hills rises steeply behind a series of
pleasant little houses of more or less Elizabethan design. It was
in one of these that the Elgars were to live for the next few years.

Edward called the place Craeg Lea and and challenged me to
guess how he had found the name. But by some stroke of luck
I realized that the key lay in the unusual spelling of 'Craeg' and
immediately saw that the thing had been built up anagrammati-
cally from (A)lice (C)arice and (E)dward Elgar. I think he was a
little annoyed that this mystification had fallen flat.

The Elgars were now on the up-grade; but W. H. Reed (who
did not know them at this time) is quite wrong in saying that
Edward was 'a popular figure and sought after for society functions and by hostesses who liked to have famous artists, poets
and musicians to add distinction to their parties'. Edward's
gifts were not social, and although he made a large number
of friends of the kind who could understand him he never fitted
well into a large mixed party. It is true that with his inevitable
over-valuation of social distinction he should be quite as sus-
ceptible as the rest of us to the attraction of great names and
the importance that friendship with their owners conferred;
but his concern with himself and his music was far too concentrated to allow him any chance of a merely social success.

The *Enigma* safely launched, he now turned his attention to
the completion of the Song Cycle *Sea Pictures* for the Norwich
Festival of the same year (1899). Perhaps it was because he had
enjoyed writing the variations and their first performance had
been taken out of his hands by an experienced conductor that
for once he did not feel exhausted after the production of a great
work. But whatever the reason, he plunged into the new enterprise with enthusiasm.

Opinion, both contemporary and subsequent, regarding the
merit of these five songs has been much divided. Mr Ernest

Newman sadly compared Edward's unskilled treatment of words with Hugo Wolf's respect for them, and few later critics have found the *Sea Pictures* wholly satisfactory. A majority view would be perhaps that while the orchestral accompaniment is always vividly illustrative, the vocal line is sometimes weighed down by the inadequacy of the words, yet sometimes transcends it.

Of the first performance at Norwich I can say nothing from my own experience as I was unable to be present; but R. H. Mottram has given us in his book about the old Bank House[1] an amusing glimpse of the Elgars at this Festival which is wholly characteristic. Mr Mottram tells us that in addition to Edward's song cycle and the Meditation from *Lux Christi*, there was to be a first performance of German's *The Seasons*, and that speculation had run high as to which work would make the deepest impression.

The Elgars had been invited to stay at the Bank House with 'J.M.' the delightful old character who is the subject of Mr Mottram's book. In the night before the performance of *Sea Pictures* was due, Mrs Elgar knocked at J.M.'s door at about 2 a.m. to ask if a doctor could be called as her husband was 'so ill'.

'"J.M.",' says Mr Mottram, 'bundled into his camlet cape and trousers and was half-way down the stairs when she came after him charmingly apologetic. Mr Elgar felt better.

'"J.M." bowed politely, holding tight to his trousers and went back to bed. Fanny thought it must have been an attack of "nerves"; but "J.M." who had never had any, didn't know what that could be. However the morning performance went off smoothly enough.'

To Mr Mottram we are indebted also for an excellent description of Edward's appearance at this time when conducting. 'His distinguished hollow-chested figure' was 'rather that of a hawk dreaming poetry in captivity'.

Sea Pictures was of course the great success of the meeting.

[1] *Portrait of an Unknown Victorian* (Robert Hale).

16

Gerontius

One day over the tea which always followed his teaching session at The Mount, Edward told me he had some important news. It appeared that the authorities of the Birmingham Triennial Festival were commissioning a large-scale choral work for performance at their meeting in October 1900.

Characteristically enough he seemed more troubled than pleased by this new opportunity as he had two works in mind and did not know which of them to write. On the one hand he had long wished to write an oratorio, perhaps a series of oratorios, on the subject of the events surrounding the Crucifixion; on the other he was deeply attracted by the possibilities of Newman's *The Dream of Gerontius*, of which a copy had been given to him as a wedding present.

It would have been impertinent to persuade him towards either of these projects but I felt that with a little sympathetic questioning I might help him to decide which of them he preferred and I soon found that it was *Gerontius* which really appealed to him the more. He was afraid, however, that the strong Catholic flavour of the poem and its insistence on the doctrine of purgatory would be prejudicial to success in a Protestant community. He told me in fact that Dvořák, who had planned a setting of the work for the 1888 Festival, had been discouraged from making it for this very reason.

My own view, for what it was worth, was that in the years

since 1888 Church of England opinion had changed sufficiently
to make *Gerontius*, if not innocuous, at least far less offensive
than it would have been when Dvořák had considered it. Moreover, since it was evident that Edward was burning to set it, I
felt that the chance of his composing another masterpiece was
much more important than any injury which might be done
to the susceptibilities of Birmingham. The upshot of this and
other talks was that *Gerontius* was chosen and the Crucifixion
series postponed till a later date.

Most of the actual scoring was done in the peace of the
cottage at Birchwood but it was evident that Edward was merely
crystallizing ideas which had been developing in his mind for
many years. Throughout the early months of 1900 we simply
lived *Gerontius*. We talked of little else on our walks and Edward
seemed to think of nothing else. Again and again manuscript
fragments would be brought to The Mount on the lesson days,
tried over and discussed. On these occasions Edward usually
played the piano since only he could understand the complexities
of his much-corrected score, my own share being to add on the
violin counterpoints he had written and of which he wanted
to hear the effect. Even the Worcestershire Philharmonic
Society were pressed into the service and were asked to play the
famous introduction to Part II, of which they must thus have
given the first concerted performance.

But although much of the music already existed in his mind,
there were sometimes severe difficulties in getting it into shape
and it would often happen that an awkward passage, after driving him almost to despair, would have to be abandoned in the
hope of later inspiration, to be replaced in the meantime by
something more immediately promising. To give the precise—
or even rough—order in which the numbers were composed
would be quite impossible, but Dr Vaughan Williams has drawn
attention to one detail which is wholly typical of Edward's
method of work. This is that the counter-melody used for the
Angel's Farewell is the music which has already appeared as the

setting of the chorus, *Lord Thou Hast Been our Refuge*, and the deduction is therefore drawn that the *Farewell* was actually written first. Dr Vaughan Williams claims no authority for this guess, but it is almost certainly correct.

Whatever the faults of *Gerontius* may be—and its greatest admirers must admit that there are serious variations of style and of inspiration—it contains more of the Elgar I knew than any other of his works written before or since. Gerontius's cry at the approach of death is the musical expression of the fear and misery that were never far below the surface of Edward's own thoughts, and indeed throughout the whole oratorio one is conscious of so close an identification between the music and the text that Edward's own soul seems inseparable from that of Gerontius.

The score was completed by June and sent off to Novellos' who were to publish it. The writing had been a severe trial both to Edward and his friends, but there had been interludes in which, perhaps fortunately, his mind had been taken off it. Thus on 24 January we had all gone to a concert at the Crystal Palace to hear some of Edward's work. Carreño, who was a friend of Miss Reynolds, the music mistress I had appointed at The Mount, played one of the Liszt concertos and when we met her in the interval, spoke warmly of a young violinist named Kreisler who was appearing in the same programme. Edward, who could not settle down to listening, took me aside and we walked round a remote part of the hall discussing plans while Manns's orchestra played a Beethoven symphony.

Then on 29 March Edward brought a young man named Granville Bantock to see me at The Mount. Bantock, who had had considerable success as a conductor, had played a number of Edward's works including the *Variations* and Edward had reciprocated by exerting some influence in favour of Bantock's appointment as Principal of the Birmingham and Midland Institute School of Music. My own impression was that the qualities which had established Bantock as a conductor and

composer were unlikely to be of service in the drudgery of work
at a big music school but Edward had no doubts. And indeed
the new principal kept the post for thirty-three years.

It cannot be said that Edward's mood that year was very
happy. Although *Gerontius* had been accepted for the Birmingham Festival he seemed uneasy and, as I thought, unduly pes-
simistic, about its future. Dr Swinnerton Heap, was to prepare
the choir and, not knowing then of Edward's quarrel with him
at Hanley, I felt that the singers would have mastered all the
difficulties of the new work—great as I knew them to be—when
Richter arrived to conduct it. In this I was probably justified
since, as Mr Nettel says, 'whatever Heap thought of Elgar's
manners he was too good a musician not to admire his music'.
But what none of us foresaw was that Heap, who had severely
overtaxed his strength, would suddenly die in May—long before
the parts of *Gerontius* had been delivered to the choir. This was
the first of the reverses with which the preparation for the performance was met.

Something clearly was needed to divert Edward's mind from
his worries and it came in a rather unexpected form. During the
nineties there had set in a craze for bicycling only comparable
with the craze for motoring of the early years of the present
century. In Malvern, where fashions were apt to be a little late,
cycling, if not actually introduced, was at any rate advertised
extensively by Lady Harberton, a local eccentric who wore
'rational dress' consisting of a shirt-blouse and bloomers of
extravagant cut in which she careered about the district on
what was elegantly described as a lady's roadster.

Having myself succumbed to the craze (but not the bloomers)
I had often suggested that it would be good for Edward's health
and perhaps happiness if he also bought a bicycle, but his natural
timidity had made it seem improbable that he would ever do so.
In the summer of 1900 however, I went cycling with some
cousins to Scotland where we had a thrilling time which was
duly reported to Edward by letter. The result was that when I

returned to Malvern I found that he had bought a bicycle which
he had been taught to ride by Mr Little of Birchwood and on
which at the first opportunity he wobbled round to The Mount
with the suggestion that I should go for a ride with him.

I asked whether Alice had been induced to follow his example and found she had not. It seemed that, feeling she would
never be able to balance on two wheels, she had hired a tricycle,
had turned a corner too fast with the result that she had fallen
off and had forsworn further attempts. This left open to Edward
and myself a field of which we took considerable advantage. Our
first afternoon was not a success for, encountering Lady Haber-
ton in Abbey Road, he was so overwhelmed that he described
a few elaborate flourishes and collapsed with a tinny crash. But
before long he had gained confidence and skill and we began a
series of explorations that were to last for many years. Of these
there will be more to say later. But their start had given a little
relief between the tensions of composing *Gerontius* and of its
first performance.

That this first performance was a failure is known to everyone. But accounts of what happened differ so widely from each
other and indeed from the facts as I saw them at the time that an
unbiased statement by an eye-witness is clearly due. (As an example of the difficulty facing historians who were not present,
one may cite on the one hand Sir Arnold Bax who in *Farewell My
Youth* quotes Elgar as saying that Richter never knew the score,
and on the other Mr F. Bonavia who tells us that Richter knew
the work by heart but rehearsed it too long and over-tired the
choir.)

In the first place it must be realized that *Gerontius* was so
utterly unlike what the choir had previously known and were
probably expecting that they not only failed to recognize that
it was a masterpiece; they did not see that it had any merit at
all. In the light of later knowledge this may seem to show incredible stupidity but one must remember that their previous
experience had been confined to hearty works of the calibre of

Messiah and, moreover, that Edward himself had hitherto written absolutely nothing of this kind. When, in consequence, they were asked to sing a work which required a deep musical insight and a subtle choral technique that even today are often beyond the scope of festival choirs, they were completely baffled and nearly refused to sing it. It would have been better had they done so, for the half-hearted and grudging treatment they gave was far worse than no performance at all.

Secondly, there was no one to give them a lead in the matter of appreciation. Dr Swinnerton Heap was dead and his place was taken by the veteran Stockley, an elderly Birmingham musician in whose orchestra Edward had once played and who had given the first performance of the *Serenade Mauresque*. Much has been made of Stockley's Nonconformity but it is probable that this would not have prevented his appreciating a Catholic masterpiece had he not been weighed down by age and infirmity.

Mrs Evans of Wolverhampton, a lady who actually sang in the choir and whose extreme candour makes her a valuable corroborative witness, remembers that the Wolverhampton contingent of the choir first heard of Dr Heap's death on the station platform when they were leaving for a rehearsal and she says that the news, as might be expected, cast a terrible gloom over the party. From the fact that Heap died in the May it is evident that rehearsals had begun in good time, yet the copies of *Gerontius* did not arrive till late in August.

Stockley, Mrs Evans describes as a pathetic figure unable to bear the strain even of standing for the long periods required. Again and again he had to rest and eat sweets to keep himself going. The rehearsals were so ruthlessly shortened that sometimes the Wolverhampton party felt resentful at having taken the twelve miles' journey for so little result. With great honesty she admits that she did not herself realize the importance of *Gerontius* till afterwards—which as neither the chorus-master nor, the soloists appreciated it either, was not surprising. Mr Nettel believes that it was not so much Stockley who wrecked the preparation as 'a poor joke, starting among some irresponsible young male choristers and spreading to the others'. Asked what this joke was, Mrs Evans said that it arose from the Demons' Chorus in Part II and one can see that to young people who had not grasped the greatness of the main work this rather ridiculous chorus, by far the weakest thing in the whole oratorio, might well be an excuse for giggling.

The rehearsals were thus carried out in such an atmosphere of bewilderment, irritation and even levity, that when Richter arrived he found himself confronted with a choir who simply did not know the work they were required to sing and who apparently had no intention of learning it. Matters had not been helped by a visit to one of the practices paid by Edward who, very naturally and justifiably enraged by the incompetence of the singing, had expressed himself forcibly on the subject and flung out of the hall. At the last rehearsal however, he sadly shook hands with everyone concerned.

The statement that Richter did not know the score seems impossible to support. He was one of the leading conductors of the day, he was a German, extremely thorough and the very last man to undertake to direct a work he did not know. Moreover he was allowed by Edward to conduct a performance of the same work at another Birmingham Festival some years later. Mr Nettel says that 'Richter had a high opinion of *Gerontius* and did his best to secure a sympathetic interpretation' but what may be doubted is whether he understood it. For one must realize that he had made his name as an exponent of the German classics (the only classics in his view) and of Wagner, whose broad effects he well knew how to handle. But whether he was the ideal interpreter of Edward's very personal vein of religious mysticism or of the strangely ethereal quality which informs much of *Gerontius*, in particular the finale, may be very much doubted.

We see then that Edward's habitual belief in forces which actively opposed his success was for once almost justified. All

the apparent advantages, a first rate choir and a famous conductor, turned into handicaps of the worst kind. But the final
blow to what success might have survived came from the soloists.

These had been chosen, as soloists at a big festival had to be
in those days when the artist was prized high above the music
he sang or played, for their box-office appeal rather than for
any very profound understanding of unfamiliar works. For
many years after she was past her best it was considered impossible to make a festival pay unless Albani were engaged. On
this occasion the singers who fell to Edwards' lot were Edward
Lloyd, Plunket Greene and Marie Brema, not one of whom
could be considered really suitable for the music to be sung.

When the day of the concert arrived then (3 October) we
went over to Birmingham in a rather sober frame of mind,
earnestly hoping for the best but not very sanguine that it would
be realized. Many of Edward's friends were there including
Miss Dora Penny and some of the other *Enigma* subjects. Jaeger,
whose immense admiration for *Gerontius* is shown in the long
appreciative analysis which he wrote for the performance, had
brought Dr Julius Buths, the German conductor who had already introduced the *Variations* to Germany and whose presence
on this occasion was to have even more far-reaching results.

The overture which announces the main themes went off so
smoothly that one breathed a sigh of relief, hoping that one's
anxiety had been unnecessary but when Edward Lloyd entered
with what should have been the heartrending cry of the dying
man it was clear that he was not only ill at ease but completely
out of rapport with the means by which Edward had expressed
Gerontius's spiritual struggle. Lloyd was a lyric tenor well able
to sustain so straightforward a part as that of Olaf but with no
understanding whatever of anything more profound than *I'll
Sing Thee Songs of Araby* into which one almost expected him to
burst at any moment. Had he done so, I thought, it might have
been some relief for he would at least have understood what he
was doing.

Before the end of the *Kyrie* it was evident that the chorus did not know the parts they were trying to sing and as the music became more chromatic, they slipped hideously out of tune. It was appalling—far far worse than one had thought possible. Those of us who knew the score and the lofty aims Edward had had in writing it suffered agonies as we thought of the misery it must be causing him and did not dare to look at him.

Gerontius is a relatively short work, for Edward only set about four hundred of the poem's nine hundred odd lines, but that first performance seemed to continue for an eternity. Why, I wondered, must Richter take the whole thing so slowly? Was he trying to underline the solemnity of the occasion? If so, I felt, he had chosen the worst possible means. Suddenly there was the dramatic pause which follows Gerontius's death and I waited for the ringing cry of the Priest whose 'Proficiscere' should, as I knew, sound like a trumpet call. But here again there was a ridiculous anticlimax for Plunket Greene, despite the immense reputation he was later to earn—and deserve—for interpretation had anything but a strong voice and was always uncertain in intonation.

At last we came to the end of the first part.

The second, which is of course a good deal longer, did little to mitigate the bad effect already made. The *Demons' Chorus* sounded like something out of a pantomime and only Marie Brema as the Angel appeared to have any grasp of the emotions the music was supposed to express. But even Mme Brema, a goddess from Valhalla if ever there was one, seemed unsuited for her part, and had she made the most brilliant success of it, she could not have saved a performance which had been hopelessly wrecked by the choir, whose pitiful stumblings indeed remained the outstanding impression. There were times when they seemed to be a whole semitone out and when the orchestra, disregarding the directions on the score, would play fortissimo in order to drag them back to the true pitch. The whole thing was a nightmare.

'This is the best of me,' Edward had written, quoting Ruskin, on the autograph score, 'for the rest I ate and drank, and slept, loved and hated, like another; my life was the vapour and is not; but this I saw and knew: this, if anything of mine, is worth your memory.'

Yet his friends knew as they rose and left the hard seats of the Town Hall that the work of which he had written these words lay in ruins from which it might never recover. Afterwards at the Queens Hotel we did what we could to cheer and encourage him. Buths, unlike most of the critics, had realized the stature of the work and spoke warmly of its great qualities. But nothing we could say was of much avail. For the time at any rate poor Edward was a broken man and only time could heal the injury he had suffered.

The one person who was not in the least disturbed was Richter. Having on that same day given a performance of *Hiawatha* which had distressed its composer only a little less than *Gerontius* had distressed Edward, the great conductor went home and finished the day with a rousing performance of the Tannhäuser overture on the pianola.

17
Cycling Days

It was evident that the failure of *Gerontius* had depressed
Edward far more than the success of the *Variations* had exhilar-
ated him. And indeed that failure seemed extraordinarily complete. Not only had the audience shown indifference; even the
press had failed to see that it was a work of any outstanding
quality and condemned it almost unanimously. Mr Nettel has
made the interesting point—and there is no doubt he is right—
that this condemnation was really intensified by the revolt,
which was then setting in amongst those who wished to see a
genuine English musical renaissance, against German domina-
tion. The appointment of Richter to the conductorship of the
Hallé Orchestra had been bitterly resented yet it was he who
had sponsored the *Variations* and *Gerontius*, and one may add
that most of Edward's other supporters at this time—Jaeger,
Buths, Ettling and Rodewald—were Germans. Whatever the
cause, there was no doubt of the ferocity of the notices, many
of which attacked not the music itself but the text. Thus it was
said, as Mr Bonavia recalls, 'to stink of incense and to offend
men and women who did not share the composer's faith.' This
of course was entirely beside the point. The real question was
whether the musical setting deepened the sense of Newman's
words and the consensus of later opinion has been that it certainly did. Most of the adverse criticism however arose not
from any real objection to the music as such, but from the very

success with which the music illustrated an unacceptable poem.

Our cycling trips began in earnest after the production of
Gerontius at Birmingham and there is no doubt that they did
Edward an immense amount of good. There is, perhaps, nothing
like physical exercise to dissolve one's worries and our exploration of the three counties of Worcester, Gloucester and Hereford not only took him away for a time at any rate, from the
tiresome problems of his work but brought him in touch with
a larger stretch of the countryside which he loved and in which
he had always found inspiration.

There cannot have been a lane within twenty miles of Malvern that we did not ultimately find. We cycled to Upton, to
Tewkesbury, to Hereford, to the Vale of Evesham, to Birtsmorton where Cardinal Wolsey is said to have fallen asleep and
come under the fatal shadow of the Ragged Stone, to the lovely
villages on the west side of the Hills—everywhere. Much of
Edward's music is closely connected with the places we visited
for, as we rode, he would often become silent and I knew that
some new melody or, more probably, some new piece of
orchestral texture, had occurred to him. Unlike most composers
he carried no notebooks in those days but seemed able to
register and remember his musical ideas even in the middle of a
conversation. On one of these occasions I offered to stop talking
in order that he might the better concentrate.

'No', he said dreamily, 'I like your vain bibble-babble.'

Some of our favourite places are mentioned in the scores of
his works and there are many more which might have been.
Longdon Marsh, near Birtsmorton, inspired much besides *The
Apostles* in the full score of which it is mentioned, and indeed if
Malvern itself always brings to my mind the *Enigma Variations*
there is hardly a turn in the roads round the town which does not
recall some passage in the early works.

Sometimes we would talk, sometimes we would pedal along
in silence. He was very difficult and one never quite knew what

would be the mood of the afternoon. There were times when
he was gay and hopeful especially at the beginning of the cycling
season when the fresh green of the trees seemed an invitation
to take longer and longer rides and he was thankful for release
from the winter confinement indoors. I found that he was particularly touched by birdsong and that he loved and knew all the
little creatures that darted in and out of the hedges. The only
occasion when he was distressed by anything he heard was one
hot afternoon when some village children in squeaking shoes
came scrunching along a rough road past the gate on which we
were resting. The unpleasant noise worked on his nerves to
such an extent that I almost expected an explosion of rage.

Our favourite rides were in the lovely country that surrounds
the southern part of the hills. We made a point of visiting all
the churches, many of which are ancient and of rare architectural
interest. I soon found that Edward, being a Catholic, had always
felt rather an outsider in matters concerning the Church of
England, in which he took an enormous interest. He had indeed
a very good knowledge of our church history and also of the
Protestant Bible which helped him in preparing the text of his
next two oratorios.

Often when we had ridden for some time in silence he would
say, 'Stop and get off, I want to talk.'

And against the spectacular background of, perhaps, Castle-
morton Common and the hills he would discuss with me at
enormous length the works on which he was engaged and
would sometimes explain with pride the ingenuity of his technical devices—with the result that we would sometimes argue
as to their merit since I could not see that ingenuity, for its own
sake and inaudible to the listener, had much value. But the
arguments were usually quite good natured.

At other times they were not. Cycling, especially in a hill
country, is often arduous work and no doubt my temper as well
as his would sometimes be to blame. On one occasion we had
taken with us as an addition to the party two neighbours whose

conversation irritated him and, to make matters worse, a drizzle of rain overtook us.

'Oh I can't stand this,' Edward suddenly exclaimed in exasperation. 'Let's go home!' And without waiting for us he turned back. We paid no attention to him and continued our ride. Relations with him were strained for a few days after that.

In general, however, we understood one another fairly well; so well indeed that as time went on he began increasingly to tell me of the misery which clouded a large part of his life. It was a tragic story of ungovernable resentment and at first I could not understand the cause, for he had a devoted wife and it was obvious that he was a rising man. But I have since realized that this resentment was obsessive and that it existed in its own right as a result of the circumstances touched in Chapter 5 and quite independently of the apparent causes in his later life. He never outgrew it.

The resentment found several channels for expression. He complained that he had not had an academic training and that those who had, the 'academics' as he contemptuously called them, were jealous of him and in conspiracy against his success. Again—a persistently recurring theme—he was short of money, and recognition, in so far as it had come at all, had come 'too late'. On one occasion he did actually burst into tears because he was convinced that he would never see some particular work printed in full score.

But the real source of his bitterness lay deeper down and was not disclosed for many months. Then one day some chance remark of mine suddenly laid bare the cruel secret. The core of the trouble, the festering sore from which there was no escape was that he was the son of a tradesman and had been brought up in a shop.

I could scarcely believe my ears. I knew that he was the son of old Mr Elgar who did in fact keep a shop in Worcester High Street and that this shop with its scores and its instruments had been the only academy Edward had ever attended. But he had made so good a use of his opportunities that many theory-bound musicians might have envied him his unusual background. That he could possibly feel ashamed of having graduated from such a school seemed fantastic and I said so. He told me with a concentrated bitterness I have never forgotten that I did not know what sort of a social handicap it was to be the son of a tradesman.

It is certain that at some time he had suffered a humiliation so cruel and so crushing that he could not bear ever to speak of it, a humiliation that arouses one's indignation at the stupidity which could have inflicted it. The tragedy was that Edward, not being intuitive about the true sources of his feelings, and prejudices, never even in later life saw the matter in its true proportion and allowed it in consequence not only to cause him deep suffering but to distort his sense of values.

Unfortunately his marriage did little to correct the distortion for while Alice would never of course, have emphasized the inferiority of Edward's social background she came from the class which had done so and had herself suffered at their hands. At the outset her very real devotion to Edward had been put to a severe test since, as we have seen, many of her friends had regarded him as socially impossible and had proceeded to cut her. To some women this might not have mattered but poor Alice with her Anglo-Indian training and rigid ideas of caste was not accustomed to being a social pariah and resented it bitterly. What made matters worse was that, much as she was hurt by her former friends' attitude to her husband, she herself really accepted the standards on which it was based and showed a certain anxiety to justify herself as the wife not merely of a genius but of a gentleman. In these circumstances she was unlikely to feel much sympathy for the social life of the music shop and in fact refused to have anything to do with it or with her husband's relatives. This was natural enough but it did nothing to counteract Edward's feeling of social inferiority.

By the time I met him therefore, there were a good many

conflicts in Edward's life and although the cycling did something to alleviate them by providing a temporary release it
obviously could not resolve them. Always at the end of the ride
he knew that he must return to the world from which, for a
time, he had escaped. The immanence of that world sometimes
spoiled even the ride.

He himself was vaguely conscious of the conflicts without
understanding them. Once when we were walking up a hill,
a tramp approached, sat on a felled tree and, taking some bread
and cheese from his pocket, began a meal. 'That man is happy,'
said Edward, 'how I envy him!' This seemed to me rather naïve
since the only thing the tramp had which Edward had not was
an acceptance of life as it came.

18

Cambridge and Llangranog

It was perhaps inevitable that Edward should have formed a rather unhappy attitude to the great musical academies. The origins of his dislike are no doubt to be found in the circumstances of his boyhood when the academies were naturally coupled in his mind with wealth, superiority and everything else that seemed exasperatingly unattainable, but he had in adult life some excuse for a certain contempt. He had after all succeeded in writing music the vitality and originality of which were often lacking in the works of the composers the schools had produced, and when Jaeger taught him the phrase 'Kapellmeister music' he applied it mercilessly to the works written by those composers for the various festivals. But his apologists seem to go much too far in claiming that this contempt was reciprocated. We have seen that it was Parry who showed the *Enigma Variations* to Richter and Stanford who first mentioned them to Mackenzie. It may be that the academies did not appreciate Edward at his true worth; his qualities were not on the whole academic qualities. But it is absurd to pretend that he was completely neglected. Moreover, when official recognition came he was strangely loth to accept it.

One day at about the time of the *Gerontius* fiasco I called at Craeg Lea and found Alice worried and upset. When I asked what was the matter she told me that Eddu had received the offer of a doctorate *honoris causa* from Cambridge University and

was on the point of refusing it. Would I go up and have a word
with him?

When I reached the study with its magnificent view of the
Severn Valley and Bredon Hill I found Edward in a state of
misery and rage. Almost without speaking he handed me the
letter from the university. I read it and said I thought the offer
delightful and a great compliment. Edward, it appeared, thought
differently. In fact he seemed to regard it as almost an insult.

I was quite unable to understand this and asked what he
meant.

'It's too late,' he said, 'I shall refuse it.'

I could not see why it should be too late but I did see in a
sudden flash that the offer might be an embarrassment. For
years Edward had complained of non-recognition and of the
hostility of the 'academics' yet here was Cambridge, where of
course Stanford was the moving spirit, offering the greatest
honour in its gift. I could understand a certain feeling of foolish-
ness but it seemed to me that he would put himself in the wrong
for ever if he refused the doctorate and I set to work to persuade
him as gently as I could to reconsider his decision.

To have argued would of course have been fatal but I pointed
out that it was rather a serious matter to snub a great university
which was offering such a distinction.

'After all,' I said, 'they are offering you all they have to give.
It will mean the pleasantest form of public recognition.'

With the childish inconsequence that was sometimes lovable
and sometimes maddening, he said that he could not afford it.

'A doctor's robes are enormously expensive,' he said, and
added a little comically, 'You have to wear a velvet cap.'

I explained patiently that this was a wholly imaginary
difficulty that the university was quite accustomed to im-
pecunious graduates and that one could always hire robes for
the day.

It seemed to me that he was weakening so I attempted no
further persuasion but left him. I believe that pressure from

several other friends—particularly Rodewald of Liverpool—
had to be applied before he would accept the doctorate, but
ultimately, to our relief, he gave in.

A few days later he told me that he had been offered a choice
of days for the ceremony and asked me to say which I thought
the most propitious. Since one of them happened to be St
Cecilia's Day, the choice was easy.

As the time approached it became clear that he had had
another motive for threatening to refuse. This, with which it
was impossible not to sympathize, was his shyness of having to
take part in a public ceremonial amongst strangers. In the end,
however, he managed to face it. The difficulty of the robes had
been overcome by the generosity of friends who subscribed to
present them to him.

When he returned to Malvern I found that he had enjoyed
his visit. The honour had been shared by Cowen, for whom at
that time Edward had a certain affection and regard, and it was
evident that he had been treated, as might have been expected,
with great tact and courtesy. In particular he had been delighted
with an especially happy quotation from the *Aeneid* in the
address of the Public Orator (Dr Sandys).

The Cambridge ceremony was the last event of much importance to Edward during 1900. The year had brought a few
successes, but he was still weighed down by the disappointment
over *Gerontius* and we all turned to the New Year hoping to see
the judgement of Birmingham and the English critics reversed
and some additional masterpiece take shape.

The first of these hopes was justified; the second was not.
On 7 February Dr Buths gave the *Enigma Variations* at
Düsseldorf and eleven days later Sir Henry Wood conducted
the Prelude to *Gerontius* and the *Angel's Farewell* in a way which
according to Jaeger 'put Richter completely in the shade'. From
the same source we learn that Colonne had heard, and been
charmed by, the *Variations* and on 9 May the Worcestershire
Philharmonic Society gave a performance of the bulk of

Gerontius which, so far as it went, seems to have given satisfaction. The most important step forward however was the production of the complete work at Düsseldorf by Dr Julius Buths.

This performance for which Dr Buths himself made a German translation of the English text was not so successful as the later one given at the Lower Rhine Festival in 1902 but it was far better than anything that had been done in England and it turned the tide of opinion in favour of the work at home. Edward and Alice stayed in Düsseldorf with the Buths family who later visited Malvern.

In the meantime Edward's fame as a composer was leading to his being asked increasingly to conduct his work at concerts. Unfortunately, however, the day of the virtuoso conductor had not yet arrived and the fees offered to him, when they were offered at all were often miserably inadequate. This annoyance lasted for the greater part of his life and as late as 1928 he wrote a letter to Sir Herbert Brewer expressing very justifiable wrath at having been asked to conduct in so great a city as Bristol for an expenses fee.

In the matter of new composition the year 1901 showed a rather serious falling off so far as quality was concerned. It seemed as if the enormous effort of writing *Gerontius* had drained his inspiration dry for a time. Of the works composed that year only three have survived in performance, the *Cockaigne* overture and the first two *Pomp and Circumstance* marches.

The overture, as its rather fanciful title indicates, was suggested by a day in London but, despite its programme—the lovers strolling in Regents Park (not St James's Park as is generally supposed) the military band, the Salvation Army procession, the church scene and so forth—it contained very much more of a certain facet of Edward's character than of London's. What was disturbing after the splendour and loftiness of *Gerontius* was that the tunes in *Cockaigne* had a tinny, rather dowdy quality and that even the love-theme hardly saved the overture from falling, as Mr Dunhill has said, between the two stools of popular appeal and studied musicianship. The orchestration, however, was, as always, a delight.

The *Pomp and Circumstance* marches have been the subject of so much controversy that one hesitates to add to it but a point may perhaps be made in regard to the quality of the trio of No. 1. This is the tune of course which with words added by A. C. Benson was later incorporated in the *Coronation Ode* for Edward VII and then published as a song with the title of *Land of Hope and Glory*. Defending this tune against the criticism it aroused, W. H. Reed said, 'Many people are unable to understand how a musician of Elgar's calibre could descend to the writing of a plain honest tune which the man in the street can sing or whistle.'

It does not seem to have occurred to Reed that the objection to *Land of Hope and Glory* might be that, unlike much that the man in the street can whistle, it was really a poor tune made infinitely worse when heavy contraltos got hold of it and sang it at a tempo far slower than that of the march. And indeed no tune the principal phrase of which works steadily down the scale can possibly produce an effect of hope, whatever it may achieve in the way of glory. *Land of Hope and Glory* came in for much criticism, but though Edward himself described it as 'a damned fine tune,' he seems in later life to have had some qualms. About twenty years afterwards at Severn House, when he was showing me one of the series of magnificent gramophones with which Mr. Gaisberg of *His Master's Voice* kept him supplied, he selected a record and said, 'Now I'll play you something thoroughly vulgar.'

What the machine proceeded to spout forth was a setting for full chorus and orchestra of *Land of Hope and Glory*.

Did he think it vulgar or was he merely bitter? I never knew.

If the music written in 1901 was not up to Edward's highest standard there was nevertheless an experience in the summer in which he found the germ of one of his greatest masterpieces.

In August I took a house at Llangranog, a seaside village in Cardiganshire to which, thankful for the change from school, I retired for a few weeks with my mother, sister and South African nephews and nieces. The holiday in this remote and inaccessible spot (Henllan, the nearest station, was fourteen miles off) was one of those rare and lovely spells that one remembers for a lifetime. The house, which was next door to the inn, stood on the edge of the shore looking across the bay in which at low tide there appeared the charmingly named island of Ynis Lochtyn.

One day a letter came from Edward and I realized that he was in one of his moods of black depression. I therefore wrote by return and suggested that he should join us. We could not put him up but rooms were available in a neighbouring cottage and it would be possible for him to come to us for meals. He accepted.

The sudden change of scene and company completely banished the depression and when he arrived, having been driven down the dark valley at night in the farmer's cart we had sent for him, it was with the air of a man who has passed through a great and exciting adventure.

As at Munich—and indeed whenever he escaped from the too artificial milieu which was at once his gaol and his goal— he showed the sunniest side of his character and was delighted with everything, the scenery, the meals of Welsh mutton and vegetables which we bought from the cottagers, above all with the sea. He had been abroad of course many times but had never I think stayed before by the seaside and it seemed to fascinate him. He had no bathing suit so we made him one out of an old pair of pyjamas; the children, with whom he made great friends, laughed and danced round him when he ventured into the water and he was not offended when one of them told him with shattering candour that he looked like a monkey.

After days spent in wandering over the hills, bathing or merely sitting in the sun, he would come in to supper and the men of the village would lounge against the seawall until someone hummed a note. Then, taking this as their key-basis they would break into a hymn in four part harmony.

The incident which made this holiday particularly memorable occurred one afternoon when we were out walking. We were on the seashore when we heard a sound of distant singing. At first we did not realize where it came from but presently noticed a group of people, on the hillside across the bay. At that distance no melodic line could be identified but one could distinguish the very frequent drop of a third, often a minor third, to which Edward drew my attention as typical of Welsh music. The singing heard in this way had a strangely ethereal beauty which deeply impressed us both and which remained in Edward's mind for many years.

Later when he wrote his *Introduction and Allegro* for string quartet and string orchestra he translated the effect of the hillside singing into a melody and used it as the second subject of that work.

19

Success

Early in 1902 Edward called at The Mount to tell me that he had had lunch with Harry Higgins of the Covent Garden Opera and had been invited to write a choral contribution to the gala performance at that theatre in honour of the coronation of Edward VII in the forthcoming June. This was the kind of occasion which always fired Edward's enthusiasm (without however necessarily inspiring his best work) and he now retired as far as possible from public life in order to compose the *Coronation Ode*. He had in Mr A. C. Benson not only a scholarly but a helpful and considerate collaborator who indeed went so far, for the final number, as to reverse the usual procedure and fit words to music already in existence as the trio of the first *Pomp and Circumstance* march. The original version of what ultimately became the song, *Land of Hope and Glory* was the result.

Once again I was to see the constituent parts of an Elgar work before hearing the whole, for he showed me many of the details at The Mount before putting them together. I did not think it and have never thought it, one of his happiest productions and I certainly never foresaw that, when ultimately it was produced, *Land of Hope and Glory* would not only achieve a triumph but be championed by many as an improvement on and suitable successor to the National Anthem. The *Coronation Ode* was completed by the end of March. It had been composed

at a white heat and had not had the benefit of the self-criticism
that Edward applied to his finest works.

Its subsequent history was almost as unlucky as that of
Gerontius. The first rehearsal took place at Queen's Hall on 14
June the Coronation having been fixed for 26 June. Edward,
having supervised this rehearsal did not remain in London but
came back to Malvern to stay until the eve of the performance.
He was now in the state of depression which always overtook
him during the period between the completion and the performance of a new work and we went for numberless cycle
rides to take his mind from its obsession. On 24 June, two days
before the Coronation, we visited Stretton Grandison, a village
just off the old Worcester–Hereford main road, where there is
a fine church. It had been a hot day and after our usual examination of the church we managed to get some tea at the inn. This
ride was to mark the end of our outings for the time being as
on the next day Edward and Alice were to go up to town for
the festivities.

Edward was already very full of the affair, the importance of
the occasion and of the Court Dress he was to wear, while conducting the Ode. On an impulse I said as we ate our simple tea,
'Does it strike you that the King is going to have an extremely trying time these next few days?'

Edward agreed that to attend a gala performance immediately after reviewing the fleet at Spithead—a trying affair
indeed with the glare of the sun and the booming of the guns—
followed by a train journey, might prove a strain to one who,
like the King, was known not to be strong.

'I think you'll find that he'll do it though,' he said.

A few minutes later the innkeeper's wife burst upon us with
the news that the King had been taken seriously ill and that the
Coronation and, in consequence, all the celebrations, had been
postponed *sine die*.

It was a terrible disappointment for Edward who once again
had to face the shattering of bright hopes, and we returned

home in gloomy anticipation of the blow which must of
necessity fall on poor Alice. She was in fact the worse sufferer
of the two as she had no satisfactory outlet for her misery,
whereas Edward found consolation in action. During the next
few days we covered an enormous distance on our bicycles.

The *Coronation Ode* did not achieve a public performance till
many months later at Sheffield and afterwards at a Queen's Hall
concert arranged by Sir Henry Wood as a national thanksgiving
for the King's recovery. The *Ode* was the outstanding success
of the evening and by general demand was repeated a few days
later at a second concert.

Work on the *Coronation Ode* and the hopes, fears, exaspera-
tions, disappointments and ultimate success attendant on its
performance lasted almost throughout 1902, but the year was
chequered by a large number of events, some happy, some less so.

In the matter of composition the only other work of importance written during the early part of the year was a pair of
little pieces for small orchestra called *Dream Children* which,
although they are not now very often heard have a delicacy that
is curiously attractive. The title was of course taken from
Charles Lamb, a passage from whose essay of the same name
was quoted in the score.

'And while I stood gazing, both the children gradually grew
fainter to my view, receding, and still receding till nothing at
last but two mournful features were seen in the uttermost
distance which, without speech, strangely impressed upon me
the effects of speech; 'We are not of Alice, nor of thee, nor are
we children at all. . . . We are nothing; less than nothing, and
dreams. We are only what might have been . . . .'

Lamb's use of the name 'Alice' gave the passage a deep and
special significance for Edward, and I always understood that
the two pieces were to be dedicated to a certain lady who was
a friend of the Elgars. When the work was published, however,
her name did not appear and there was in fact no dedication
whatever.

In May came the second performance at Düsseldorf of
Gerontius. The first had been somewhat marred by the un-
certainty of the Angel but this blemish was completely removed
when in May the part was sung by the English contralto,
Muriel Foster. It was after this May performance that Edward
received what he himself regarded as the most important compliment of his life up to this time. It came from Richard Strauss
who at a luncheon party proposed the health of 'the first progressive English musician, Meister Elgar'. Edward, who had
an immense admiration for Strauss, was profoundly touched by
this tribute and something of a friendship sprang up between
the two composers, which was deepened when Strauss visited
London a month later. They made a pact that each should
orchestrate one of Bach's organ 'fantasies' and fugues—a pact
which only Edward kept. What is perhaps not known is that
during a discussion on possible subjects for a big work Strauss
asked for suggestions and was advised by Edward to consider
the Book of Job.

According to Edward's account given to me a few days later
at Malvern, he had been staggered to find that Strauss had
never read Job. I imagine, however, that since Strauss's command of English was not then very great and Edward's of
German was almost non-existent, the very different pronuncia-
tions of 'Job' in the two languages may have led to a misunderstanding.

It was undoubtedly the success of these two Düsseldorf per-
formances that brought home to festival committees in England
the fact that *Gerontius* was a work of genius. In 1901 the only
English performance—an incomplete one—had been that by
Edward's own club, the Worcestershire Philharmonic Society.
But in 1902 performances were given in both the Three Choirs
and Sheffield Festivals to be followed within a few months by
others all over England and in many European cities. The
Gerontius of the Three Choirs (meeting at Worcester) was
John Coates who thus made his first appearance in a part with

which he was to be identified for many years and of which he became one of the greatest exponents.

This sudden turning of the tide in favour of *Gerontius*, and more particularly its success on the Continent, had a very beneficial effect on Edward which showed itself in his bearing in public. For years he had never cut a very successful or distinguished figure on the platform. As a conductor he had been nervous, fidgety and in consequence ill-tempered. ('Why must he be so fierce' members of the Worcestershire Philharmonic Society would ask.) And in social intercourse he had always seemed shy or awkward or, what was worse, boisterously facetious. Someone suggested in fact that he often looked as though he owed money.

Towards the end of 1902 a marked change began to set in which was as gratifying to his friends as its cause must have been to him. This change did not mature in time to prevent the rupture with the Worcestershire Philharmonic Society but soon afterwards we noticed a greater assurance in his manner and a greater alertness and enthusiasm in his dealings with the choirs and orchestras which were willing to perform his works.

The greater happiness that this assurance implied was nevertheless tempered in 1902 by the most cruel personal loss that he ever suffered. On 1 September, only ten days before he was to conduct *Gerontius* at the Worcester Festival, his mother died. A few days earlier we had cycled into Worcester where I waited for him at a tea shop while he paid her what was to be his last visit. When he joined me he was so deeply moved that he could hardly speak, for he knew that she was dying. I have always regretted that I was never allowed to meet old Mrs Elgar since there is no doubt that she was the best influence he ever knew. To her training he owed many of his best qualities and I think it is true to say that the first bitterness of losing her coincided in his case with the beginnings of that *Weltschmerz* from which every artist seems to suffer when he has achieved what he believes to be the summit of his success.

Earlier in the year Edward had begun to plan a new large-scale work, the most grandiose indeed of his whole career as a composer. He had of course been a good deal impressed by hearing *The Ring* at Munich in 1893 and the ambition to write a work of similar proportions had long been in his mind. An operatic cycle was out of the question in England but a trio of oratorios based on the New Testament story and informed by a complicated system of *leitmotiven* in the Wagnerian manner seemed worth while attempting. Shortly after the first disappointment over the *Coronation Ode*, Edward had gone to Bayreuth and had heard both *The Ring* and *Parsifal*. Although W. H. Reed is wrong in supposing that this visit suggested the oratorio-trilogy, which had in fact taken a vague shape in Edward's mind early enough to be rejected in favour of *Gerontius*, it may be that the old ambition was revived by Bayreuth for he set to work on the new trilogy immediately on his return to Craeg Lea.

In arranging his libretto, which for the first time he himself undertook, Edward followed the plan, usual in oratorio, of fitting together extracts from the New Testament in such a way as to produce what, it was hoped, would be a connected story. This was an extremely difficult task, but he was helped by his immense interest in the Protestant Bible to which of course he had not, as a Catholic, been brought up and which fascinated him in consequence.

The trilogy was designed to cover (*a*) the events leading up to the Crucifixion and the calling of the Apostles (*b*) the founding of the Kingdom and (*c*) the coming of Antichrist and the final triumph of Christ. The first oratorio which he originally called *The Apostles* Part I, was composed in the autumn of 1902 and the beginning of 1903.

The really original feature of the oratorios was the adoption in them of Wagnerian methods. A system of *leitmotiven* was devised which was intended to knit the whole trilogy together and which, incidentally, made considerable demands on the listener's memory. Nevertheless when the opening work was performed at Birmingham at the Triennial Festival on 14 October 1903 it made a success in strong contrast to the failure of *Gerontius* at the previous festival in 1900.

This greater success, which has not been confirmed by later audiences, was due to a number of causes not all of which were to be found in the work itself. The recognition of Edward's genius in Germany—more especially by Richard Strauss—had made the Birmingham choir's failure to give *Gerontius* even a respectable performance look extremely foolish. A masterpiece had been offered them and they had treated it with contempt. By 1903, when *The Apostles* was in rehearsal, *Gerontius* had begun its long career of success and the choir were determined not to repeat their gaffe.

A second factor in the success was that, although Richter was still conductor-in-chief to the Festival, Edward decided to direct his own work himself. This was very wise. He was not, and never became, a good conductor judged from the strictly technical viewpoint; the inability to communicate knowledge which made him an unsatisfactory teacher would always have prevented his making any success as a *repetiteur* but, given a choir and orchestra that had been adequately primed, he nevertheless did inspire fine performances of his own greatest works. He himself seemed deeply moved by them and his emotion seemed, now that he had lost much of the painful selfconsciousness of earlier days, to engulf the performers and to carry them with it. A very distinguished musician who does not admire *Gerontius* joined a choir which was performing the work under Edward's own direction and confessed that, while the conducting was technically inefficient, he was completely swept away by Edward's personal magnetism.

Whatever the cause an emphatic success had been made, and Edward's stature, already greater, seemed to grow in the sun of public appreciation. Alice had persuaded him to buy a fur-lined coat in which he made an impressive figure and which had

to be worn even though the weather that October was not
particularly cold. The performance was the last Elgar première
I was to attend for some years and I enjoyed it. By some chance
I had been placed in the hall among a group of critics and
musicians and when later Edward and I went for a long cycle
ride to conduct an inquest on the performance I was able to tell
him what had been said. It had been quite obvious that Henry
Wood had been impressed, that several singers had had a busy
time tracking the soloists in the score and that Dr MacNaught
had been wondering how the thing would look in tonic sol-
fa. . . .

The Apostles survives in occasional performances but has not
repeated the success of Gerontius. It contains some of Edward's
finest music but Ernest Newman has put his finger on its main
weakness in an analysis which compares its faults to those of
Olaf. It is indeed a patchwork of texts which, however skilfully
contrived, fails for long stretches to achieve coherence. Mr
Newman was so worried by the trend which Edward's work
was taking at this time in fact that he felt obliged to tell him so.
Edward showed me what he had said and I felt it to be—as one
might expect from a critic who had supported Edward with
great devotion—completely sincere and also very tactfully
worded. Unfortunately Edward was bitterly offended and took
a line which was wholly typical. His respect for Mr Newman
was too deep for the criticism to be ignored and I think (as he
never completed the trilogy) that he secretly felt it to be just.
He therefore met it by attributing to his critic motives which
had quite certainly never existed. He pointed out that Mr
Newman was an agnostic and claimed that the purposes behind
the criticism was to make him give up his religion which, quite
without persuasion from Mr Newman, he did largely give up
in later years. This seemed to me a lamentable misconstruction
to put on the matter and I am glad to say that Edward ultimately forgave his critic.

But Alice, who regarded the least breath of criticism as
malicious, never forgave him.

20

Alassio

Despite the ever-increasing popularity of *Gerontius* in the provinces, London had not yet heard it although the work was now over two years old. A performance there was clearly overdue but when an offer finally came, it came from a somewhat unexpected quarter. Whether Edward was right or not in grumbling that his faith had been a handicap to his career it is certainly true that the Catholics had done little to help him. It may be argued that, not being in command of festival machinery such as that of the Three Choirs and the large provincial towns, and having no very large churches or choral organizations, they could give him no such help. However the first London performance was permitted in the new Westminster Cathedral. Liturgical music alone is allowed in Catholic churches and this performance, the only one ever given there, was possible only because the Cathedral was as yet unconsecrated. When it is added that the impresario who arranged matters was a Jew and that the choir chosen by Edward was the North Staffordshire District Choral Society, which consisted mainly of Dissenters it will be realized that this was hardly an exclusively Catholic occasion.

Nor was the performance a very happy one. Despite the devotion of the choir, who actually paid their own fares from Hanley, everything seemed a little unsatisfactory. The unfinished walls were acoustically dead and, although Muriel Foster repeated her Düsseldorf success as the Angel, the

German tenor, who had won Edward's admiration at both of the festivals there as Gerontius, proved a sad disappointment. The trouble was that, obliged on this occasion to abandon his native tongue and sing in English, he produced horrible distortions of our vowel-sounds which seriously endangered the gravity of the proceedings. At the outset it had seemed as if the performance would never begin at all since, through some misunderstanding, Edward was placed in one room to await the arrival of a dignitary of the church, who was to preside but who was shown into another room and left there.

The production of *The Apostles* at Birmingham coincided with a turning point in the Elgar's finances. The fee paid by the Festival Committee was the largest Edward had ever received, running, I believe, into four digits and provided an emancipation from some of the worries which had dogged him. This gradual increase in prosperity enabled him not only to give up much of his teaching but also to achieve an old ambition and spend part of the winter in Italy. On 25 November therefore he and Alice left Malvern for Alassio on the Italian Riviera.

Carice, who was still at The Mount, could not very well accompany them so long before the end of the term but when we broke up she and I followed her parents to Italy.

Edward and Alice met us at Genoa, where we all stayed the night. Once again I realized how happy Edward could be when relieved from the repressive influence of Malvern. He was overjoyed at seeing us and for a few moments it almost seemed as if Edward and Alice were the two children and Carice and I the grown-ups. The next morning was spent in Genoa and Edward, who kept darting down little side streets and alleys, to the manifest alarm of Alice, found a music-shop where he bought some orchestral manuscript paper and arranged—not without some difficulty which it was my business as interpreter to ease —for the hire of a small piano. Carice watched our antics with her usual quiet and charming gravity.

In the afternoon we reached the Villa San Giovanni, the

house they had taken at Alassio. It was not quite the pleasant
place with whitewashed walls and large sunny rooms of my
imagination but one of a number of brick-houses built for
tourists, and I soon discovered that the visit had not come fully
up to their expectations. For one thing the weather had been
cold and cheerless but what was worse than the weather was
the society.

The Elgars had lived as we have seen in a somewhat circum-
scribed milieu in Malvern, which to this day is one of the most
conventionally-minded places in the British Isles, and it may
well be that neither Edward nor Alice realized how the
permanent English colony of a place like Alassio is con-
stituted. They very soon found that the English people in the
town had settled there for the most part because either their
means or their desire for a freer life had made it better for them
to choose a place where they were not known. 'There are more
old ladies in Alassio than there are in Malvern.' Edward
grumbled and Alice was shocked by the freedom from convention of the other section of the English population. This
was exemplified by an incident that occurred soon after our
arrival. Entertaining was not of a very formal character and ran
to coffee and chocolate biscuits rather than dinner-parties. I was
not surprised therefore when a note arrived from some neighbours, asking the Elgars' party to come in one night after
dinner. Alice, however, was horrified and really seemed to
regard the invitation as an insult. When I asked why she said
indignantly.

'They've never even called on us.'

In the end I went alone and thoroughly enjoyed myself.

If the society was disappointing, the Italian countryside undoubtedly fulfilled all expectations. Again and again we would
walk up the *salitas* on the hillside to look at the glorious views
of blue sea and broken coast and to bask in the Italian sunshine
which, even in December, was bright and warm. One day on
our return we heard that the piano had arrived and we rushed

down to the station to find it standing in the Goods Depart-
ment (Sala di merci) which Edward with a flash of inspiration
called the Hall of Mercy. It was not a very large piano—the
kind that in England is handled by two men and a boy, but the
stationmaster had empanelled a jury of twelve good men and
true, all smelling of garlic who, sweating frightfully and swear-
ing even more frightfully, staggered with it up to the villa.
Edward who had a professional knowledge of the moving of
pianos regarded their efforts sardonically. . . .

When it was installed he sat down and played something that
was new to me. Like many of his tunes, it did not strike me as
being particularly good, a two-bar phrase that was repeated
sequentially *ad nauseam*. Yet it remained in my memory for many
years, until, in fact it cropped up again in circumstances which
will be described later.

One friendship the Elgars did make by unconventional
means in Alassio. On the first Sunday in the New Year I
attended service at the English Church where the lessons were
read by a strikingly handsome clergyman. That afternoon
Edward, Alice and I were sitting on the balcony at the villa,
when this same clergyman passed by. Edward was impressed
by his leonine head and commented on his superiority to the
general run of Italian priests.

Some days later Edward and Carice and I were on the hills
above the town when we suddenly came on our clergyman
walking alone. He waved an arm towards the sea and said,
'Isn't this glorious?' And without any more ado we continued
our walk together. We discovered that he was Dr J. Armitage
Robinson, the then Dean of Westminster.

This was a happy encounter since, by some lucky chance, the
two men liked each other at first sight, and only parted after
expressing a hope that they would soon meet again. This hope
Alice implemented by means of one of her polite notes inviting
the Dean to lunch. He accepted and to Edward's delight turned
out to be an authority on Biblical research, who could answer

many of the questions that had arisen in regard to the oratorio trilogy. I believe that later he gave Edward a good deal of helpful advice in regard to the second work of the set, *The Kingdom*.

The Alassio holiday brought out, as the Munich one had done ten years before, what I always felt to be Edward's most lovable quality—a schoolboyish interest in simple things.

From the balcony of the villa one had a good view of the Mediterranean and I remember Edward's joy at discovering that the fishermen were still drawing in their nets in the precise manner described by Virgil. Then again he noticed one day that some small ships had anchored in the bay and were unloading barrels of wine.

'Come here,' he shouted excitedly. 'You must see this!'

The barrels were simply being heaved overboard into the sea to be pulled ashore by stalwarts in rolled-up trousers who waded out to meet them. After this nothing would do but that I should go to the pier, interview the Customs Officer and find out where the wine came from and where it was going. I learnt that it was from Sardinia (Vino di Sardegno) and that it was delivered to a little trattoria in a side street.

It was clear that if my reputation were to be maintained I must get some of this wine so I found my way to the trattoria and went in; I did not take Edward as he tended to embarrass one's shopping by making a running commentary on the proceedings in English. ('Tell him he's a squinting pirate', he would say while one bargained.)

The principal room of the trattoria was very large and dark with a low ceiling and long tables. It looked a good setting for any imaginable wickedness. However the proprietor sold me a large fiasco of the wine, no doubt at about five times the price paid by the habitués, but even so ridiculously cheaply, and I carried it back to the villa in triumph. Edward greeted me with shouts of joy and would drink nothing else. It was strangely touching to see him so easily pleased and to realize that beneath the rather tiresome complexities of his character there lay this lovable vein of simplicity.

Another experience which he enjoyed was Midnight Mass on Christmas Eve at a little church some way inland which made a speciality of this celebration. All the local shepherds were present and there were two little lambs on the altar who bleated when 'É Nato Jesu' was sung. One wondered if their tails were tweaked to produce this effect.

At Alassio, as everywhere else, Edward's favourite exercise was walking, and on our walks Edward would be in the gayest of moods and would tease us endlessly. But sometimes there would be serious delays in starting, caused by Alice's fussiness over detail. On one occasion she exasperated him to such an extent over the preparations for a picnic that by the time she was ready he lost his temper and refused to go. We got round him in the end but it seemed unfortunate that she should put a brake on his enjoyment by her concern with the very conventions from which he most needed to escape.

The principal work inspired by this holiday was, of course, *In the South*, the third and last of Edward's concert overtures. A good deal has been written about the scenes and thoughts on which the music was based, but one or two additional points may be of interest. Mr W. H. Reed has told us that a certain much repeated three-note phase was suggested by a neighbouring place-name which took Edward's fancy so much that he was always repeating it with a kind of relish. Moglio was a village through which we often walked, a dear, dirty, little place spectacularly placed on the hillside. The minute houses were built beside and below the level of the steep *salitas* with the result that the returning inhabitants would walk rapidly down hill and suddenly disappear into their homes like rabbits into a burrow. Edward loved this and never tired of seeing them disappear.

'There one really could roll home,' someone said.

'Moglio, Moglio roglio roglio,' said Edward with a pleasing access of fatuity.

The overture is really a musical synthesis of the impressions Edward received during the holiday. He would often contemplate the fine Roman bridge over the river and the thought of Caesar's legions crossing the bridge on their way to Gaul suggested the stirring middle section. The experience which always comes to mind when I hear the overture however, is that which gave rise to the *Canto Popolare*.

One afternoon we had climbed one of the *salitas* and came suddenly upon a little chapel by a group of pine trees. Classical in style, like a temple, it was falling into ruin and the sudden impact of its beauty silenced us.

'It really only needs a shepherd with his pipe to make the picture complete,' I said.

At that moment to our amazement a shepherd did in fact appear from behind the chapel. He was dressed in a sheepskin, and unconcernedly drove his flock along the path and out of sight.

The *Canto Popolare* achieved such a success that it was issued as a separate number in various arrangements which seem to have disappeared from currency. I remember that the first time I heard the overture I was sitting next to Herbert Thompson, the then critic of the *Yorkshire Post* and that, as the *Canto* was played he whispered, 'I think this is one of the most exquisite tunes ever written.' Certainly it seemed to become to Edward an expression of all that had been happiest in the holiday.

In January I had to return to England for the beginning of the spring term but the Elgars intended to stay for at least another month. With one of those swift changes of feeling that were characteristic, however, they decided a few days later to follow. Alassio, which had seemed delightful, had suddenly lost its charm. The winds were too cold and a doctor whom Edward saw forbade him to drink any more of the Sardinian wine and advised Canadian club whisky instead, surely a strange prescription.

On 25 January they left for home.

21
Plas Gwyn

The year 1904 was marked by many honours which showed the enormous increase of Edward's prestige. The first of these, for which arrangements had been begun before his departure for Alassio at the end of 1903, was nothing less than a three-days' festival of his music in Covent Garden theatre and attended by King Edward VII and Queen Alexandra.

It is not easy, as concert promoters are aware, to arrange a satisfactory all-Elgar concert owing to a certain sameness of the music in theme and treatment. Nevertheless, the festival was an enormous success. Practically all the major choral and orchestral works written up to that time were given, including a first performance of the Alassio overture, *In the South*. The Elgars were presented to the King and Queen and were sent home with a large wreath which decorated the study for long afterwards—until, indeed its leaves were faded and brown.

Alice was unaffectedly delighted with the success of the festival. Edward was not. It had always been his just complaint that those who sought to help him performed his music but never dreamt of paying him for it. Apparently the financial side of the undertaking was unsatisfactory for he told me—not for the first time—that he had never been so insulted in his whole life.

If their cash value seemed dubious, the honours nevertheless continued to pour in. *The Apostles* was repeated at Birmingham

and given for the first time at Gloucester, Rotterdam, Mainz
and particularly Cologne where the Elgars and Jaeger attended
a memorable performance under Dr Buths. On 3 April at the
instance of Parry and Stanford, those 'academics' whom
Edward so bitterly despised, he was elected under Rule II to
membership of the Athenaeum, a distinction he prized very
highly; on 21 June he received the degree of Mus. Doc.
Dunelm, and on 6 October that of L.L.D., from the University
of Leeds; on 5 July he attended an evening party at Marl-
borough House; on 26 November he was offered the newly
founded Peyton Chair of Music at Birmingham University; and
in December he was elected to honorary membership of the
Royal Academy of Music.

It was however, on 24 June that the Elgars heard of what
was socially the greatest honour of all. Either on that day or the
next morning I received a little note from Alice asking me to
take Carice and her friend Cissie Cuthbert to tea at Craeg Lea as
there was some '*most exciting news*'. Alice liked to surround herself with a little mystery but this time the secret had leaked out
and we knew that Arthur Balfour had written asking Edward
if he would accept a knighthood.

'I expect,' said Cissie, one of those tactful little girls who
seem early marked out for a career of domestic diplomacy, 'that
we'd better call her "Lady Elgar" as many times as possible.'

The tea party, attended only, I think, by Ivor Atkins (later
to receive a knighthood himself), the two children and myself,
was a happy one. It was impossible not to feel that Edward had
fully deserved the honour, impossible not to sympathize with
Alice's pride that her husband had achieved, in addition to a
musical success, a rank, which must command the respect of
those friends who had looked down on him. But in spite of
Cissie's excellent resolve we somehow felt shy of the title and
it was Ivor who at last said, 'Well someone has to take the
plunge. May I pass you a cake *Lady* Elgar?'

One footnote may be added. I am reminded by Mrs Williams,

who was for many years parlour-maid at The Mount and who is still living in Worcester, that Carice on hearing the news said to her, 'I am so glad for Mother's sake that Father has been knighted. You see—it puts her back where she was.'

Exactly why the Elgars uprooted themselves from Malvern, in which they had lived for thirteen years, and went to Hereford, was never really made clear to their friends. The increase of their means, and of course Edward's fame, made a larger house than Craeg Lea desirable but there were plenty of large houses available in Malvern and it seemed odd at a time when Edward was needing to go more often to London that he should move farther away. Hereford, for all its charm as a city, does not compare with Malvern as a centre for the walks which were Edward's favourite form of exercise and the society of a cathedral close did not seem to be the ideal environment for a composer of genius. Could it have been that with the improvement in their social status Alice wished to remove them still further from the neighbourhood of the little music shop in Worcester?

The first I heard of the move was when on one of our cycle rides Edward suddenly said, 'They've found a house for me at Hereford.'

This was a locution he often used when he wished to disclaim responsibility for any step he had taken, but I could hardly suppose he would allow himself to be transplanted against his will and I asked no questions. Later I heard that the house had in fact been taken.

On St Peter's Day, 1904, Edward and I cycled over to see it. Despite protestations that the move would make no difference to our friendship we knew that a period in our relationship was ending and we were more than usually silent. We took the road along the east side of the hills, a road of great beauty with the wooded heights on the right side and the drop to the Severn on the left. At Little Malvern we dismounted and entered the Catholic Church in the graveyard of which Edward and Alice were both ultimately to rest. Then, refreshed by the silence, we resumed the now very familiar ride through Ledbury, with its black and white houses, and Stoke Edith into Hereford.

Plas Gwyn, the house chosen, stood (and still stands) well outside the town near the top of Eign Hill on the road which runs due east out of the city and for a time fairly close to the left bank of the Wye. Much older than Craeg Lea, it was a square house placed at the corner made by a side turning called Vineyard Road. The little property was what house agents describe as matured and well-wooded and the whole suburb attractive and spacious with charming glimpses of the Wye Valley through the trees on the opposite side of the road from Plas Gwyn but I was not on the whole favourably impressed. There were attractive features, the verandah running round two sides and partly covered with climbing plants, the relatively large rooms and the garden . . . yet to me it looked, with its two plastered sides towards the roads and its two red brick sides towards the garden (a fairly common Midland arrangement), the sort of house that might be chosen by a prosperous and aesthetically not very exacting merchant rather than a suitable home for a sensitive and highly strung artist.

However, I surveyed the four floors, one of them a semi-basement which would surely involve domestic trouble, and said I hoped Edward would find happiness there. Whether on balance he did so may be very much doubted. The implications of his conversation and of the letters which from the time of the move he began to write to me are that he did not. The local society was stuffy and slow and its dullness began soon to tell on him.

'If only you could see the frightful old fizgigs'—a favourite word of his—'who are fetched in to entertain me,' he wrote. It is undeniable, moreover, that the note of melancholy which is heard in much of his music is especially pronounced in the works written at Hereford. 'Rarely, rarely comest thou, Spirit of Delight', is the motto from Shelley of the Second Symphony and except in the case of the *Introduction and Allegro for Strings*, which probably existed in his mind as the fruit of a joyous holiday before he went to Plas Gwyn, the same quotation might be applied to almost everything he wrote at Hereford. Thus, though there is a certain effect of noble striving about the First Symphony the general tone is anything but one of happiness. The Violin Concerto, for all its wistfulness, is almost a prolonged cry of despair, the Second Symphony actually takes for its motive the lines mentioned above and *The Kingdom*, which was finished at an immense expenditure of energy, completely exhausted his ability to write oratorios with the result that the great trilogy remained incomplete.

The melancholy was by no means confined to his music. From about the beginning of the Plas Gwyn period to the end of his life he never seemed able to shake off a recurrent depression. Again and again in his letters he speaks of feeling wretchedly ill or of finding the world 'very old'.

'I seem tired, oh so tired of everything and so useless,' he wrote to me on one occasion and there were many variations on this theme.

It can hardly be said that the volume of his work fell off at Hereford but the times when his inspiration went, as he called it, 'off the boil' seemed more frequent. On these days he would throw himself into other interests which, however absorbing and perhaps necessary as a relief, often seemed a sad waste of time and energy. There was a shed in the garden, which he called the Ark, and here, with a number of test tubes, retorts and chemicals, he worked off some of the schoolboy interest in stinks and explosions which had never found expression in his all-too-limited childhood. A contributory cause of his depression was that poor Jaeger, on whom Edward had for many years depended as chief encourager, was now manifestly doomed and unable to fulfil his old function. A visit to Davos at about this time did little to arrest the disease.

Sometimes Edward would send for me and I would go over

and try to cheer him. Hereford is only fifteen miles from Malvern and at first I went to Plas Gwyn fairly often. Sometimes on our bicycles we would explore the villages in search of the churches Edward loved so much, of which a new range had been opened up by the move.

While they lasted, these rides, of which there were many, probably did some good but as time went on I felt more and more unable to cope with or to understand the steady increase of gloom. The strange part of it was that this gloom seemed to set in at precisely the moment when greater prosperity was beginning to make Edward's life, outwardly, at any rate, more comfortable. He had abandoned the hated teaching on leaving Malvern and was beginning to be a composer of world fame. An invitation to America, the first of several, arrived soon after he settled at the new home, everywhere he was being fêted and welcomed. Yet his reaction to all the signs of success were always the same. They had come 'too late'.

That this complaint was ill-judged has already been pointed out. The slowness with which recognition came was due not to neglect but to a corresponding slowness in Edward's develop-ment. When one thinks, indeed of the case of César Franck who, although he had already written some of his finest works many years previously, did not achieve popular success until he was 68—and who was then almost immediately knocked down in the street and mortally injured—one is amazed at the rapidity of Edward's progress. Almost unknown in 1898 he had by 1904 earned knighthood and the unquestioned position of leading English composer. Whatever may have been the cause of his unhappiness then, it could not really have been due to neglect and another explanation must be sought.

The present writers believe that it can only be found in the conflict of aims to which attention has already been drawn and which had become intensified as Edward grew older. On the one hand he was an artist with an artist's single-minded deter-mination to achieve the highest of which he was capable at the

expense of every competing interest. On the other, bitterly hurt
in childhood perhaps by social humiliations he was a worldling
with an insatiable appetite for wealth, position and the earthly
shows in general. Now composers do not earn large sums of
money, nor if they are sufficiently immersed in their work does
the lack of money seem to trouble them. But Edward had not
this singleness of purpose. He wanted to write great music and
did in fact succeed in writing it. But he wanted a dazzling social
success as well and was thus following two ideals which were
mutually destructive.

The two ideals were reflected in his friendships. On the one
hand there were musicians like Jaeger, W. H. Reed and the
three young cathedral organists, Atkins, Brewer and Sinclair
whose appointment pleased him on account of their devotion
and help. These men brought out, and in some cases, perhaps,
only knew, the best in him. But on the other hand there were a
number of wealthy friends whom he was proud to know but
whose effect on him seemed to be thoroughly undesirable. This
was noticed by many who had his interests at heart. Dr Colles
in *Grove's Dictionary* referred to Edward's tendency to fritter
time away over trivial people and Jaeger besought me almost
with tears in his eyes to try to discourage some of these associations.

It may well be, of course, that Jaeger, who, whether justly
or not, undoubtedly felt neglected by Edward in the later years
of success, was a little swayed by jealousy and that the new friends
were not quite so harmful as he thought them. One fact, however, is undeniable. A relatively poor but ambitious man who
is brought constantly into contact with the very rich needs a
very sure philosophy if his envy of them is not to become unbearable. The accidents of Edward's youth had tended to de-
prive him of any such philosophy and he suffered in consequence
a torment of envy which often wrecked the serenity of spirit in
which an artist needs to work.

22

Full Recognition

When the Elgars moved to Hereford they were missed less in Malvern than would have been the case but for their increasing tendency to hold aloof from local activities. But Edward had resigned from the conductorship of the Worcestershire Philharmonic Society in 1902 and, although he ultimately consented to help with the musical competitions in which Lady Mary Lygon was the moving spirit, they involved him in nothing more than an annual appearance. Even here he was not wholly happy, feeling no doubt that his dignity had sometimes been infringed and there was more than one occasion on which the adjudicator chosen by the Committee exasperated him. 'S —— is a clotted idiot,' he said of one distinguished visitor.

For me, however, the departure of the Elgars left a gap that was very difficult to fill. Whatever the differences of our outlook and opinions, we had for over ten years been on terms of the greatest intimacy and in almost daily contact, Carice indeed having since 1899 spent more time with me than with her parents. I had thus followed the rise of Edward's fortunes with something of the feeling of a member of the family. Our friendship was to last for many more years but after the summer of 1904 our meetings were more widely spaced and more concentrated in interest.

Early in 1905 I spent a few days at Plas Gwyn, having received a charmingly worded invitation in which my Christian

name had been neatly worked into the initial letter of my sur-
name. So much had happened or was in prospect that the recent
success of *The Apostles* seemed forgotten. A new work was on
the stocks; a visit was to be paid to Yale University in America;
there was the question of the lectures to be given in connection
with the University Chair at Birmingham; and the delightful
discovery had been made that one could reach a Catholic chapel
by taking a boat across the Wye at the foot of Eign Hill.

I listened to the flow of news, some of it trivial, some important, as always happens when old friends meet, but what I
was really dying to hear was the new work. I knew that Edward
would not give me any details until he felt in the right mood
and that I must wait, yet it was hard to be patient and I was glad
when at last the green linen manuscript book was produced
and the sheets arranged on the piano.

The work, of which he proceeded to give a very good sketch,
has always seemed to me, and I know to many others, his finest
single movement. From the germ of the choral singing heard
on the hillside when he had stayed with me at Llangranog he
had developed a brilliant *Introduction and Allegro* for strings. It
had been laid out, as he explained, somewhat on the lines of the
Handelian *concerto grosso* with a solo string quartet as *concertino*
and the rest of the forces as *ripieno*, but I hardly listened to his
explanation because I had been so enormously impressed by the
quality of the music itself and by the peculiarly convincing effect
of its structure. Despite the variety of its emotional content this
movement seemed to me to follow an inexorable logic of its
own and to end at the precise moment when its argument was
completed. The themes had not been forced into a mould they
did not fit, nor had they been left in an amorphous mass. The
work was in short a masterpiece.

In his analysis of Edward's duality as a composer Mr Frank
Howes plays for a moment with the idea that the Elgar who
wrote for strings generally produced a purer metal than the
Elgar who wrote for brass and it is a fact that the *Introduction and*

Allegro is almost the only work of his which has aroused practically no adverse criticism. Perhaps it may be said indeed to summarize most of his finest qualities as a composer. It has the Elgarian wistfulness without the Elgarian morbidity and this wistfulness is balanced and set off by the energy of a magnificently virile fugue. The writing for the strings is masterly.

To this may be added a footnote the triviality of which will, it is hoped, be excused on the ground that it does not seem to have been made by anyone else. All who studied the violin under Elgar will remember that he had a habit of picking up the instrument and testing it by flourishing off one or two cadences in spread chords. There are several such cadences in the *Introduction and Allegro* and, while they do not seem particularly remarkable and are played not by one violin but by the whole orchestra, they are so exactly like the flourishes he used to throw off when teaching that I never hear them without seeing him as he used to stand fiddle under chin in the music-room at The Mount. What is odder is that the work seems to call up something of his person and manner and of the way in which he used to move about the room.

Edward's occupation of the Peyton Chair at Birmingham University is one of the most difficult subjects with which his biographers have had to deal. The offer of this appointment arose from the natural desire of his friends to see him earning some share at any rate, of the income to which as the leading British composer he was entitled, but unfortunately it was made in complete disregard of his suitability or otherwise for the post.

It is perhaps obvious that a teacher, to be successful, must be able to analyse in detail the progressive steps by which he himself has acquired his technique and must be able to guide his pupils' steps along the same path. At The Mount, puzzled by his failure to do anything of this kind, I had supposed that Edward had completely forgotten these steps until it suddenly occurred to me that he had never taken them at all. Genius

evolves its own technique and Edward's had come by intuition. It is almost true to say that he was incapable of acquiring
any knowledge by a laborious process of study. He learned in a
flash of inspiration or not at all. There was thus a certain basis
of truth in his often-made and yet baffling remark that he did
not understand anything about music. If by understanding
music is meant the ability to analyse what may be called its
philosophy and metaphysics in the manner of Tovey, Edward
did not understand it. Music for him, as for Delius, was a means
of expression, not a subject for discussion. He could no more
have given Walford Davies's talks on Music and the Ordinary
Listener than Walford Davies could have written the *Enigma
Variations*.

When, therefore, he was required to deliver a series of lectures to the Birmingham students he was almost completely
at sea. It must not be supposed that he took his duties lightly
or flippantly. Except that he loathed, and sometimes refused to
undertake, the task of examining manuscripts submitted to him,
he really did his utmost to fulfil the obligation. But the fact
remained that musically he was the counterpart of those heroes
of our own day, who having achieved some monumental act of
courage and determination are utterly unable when brought to
the microphone to give anything like a coherent account of
what they have done. He would spend hours in the planning of
the lectures—hours of such agony for himself and his household
that Carice could never remember them without a shudder.
And yet the result was nearly always a hopeless muddle.

In order to prepare the inaugural address he retired to the
house of one of the wealthy friends whom Jaeger distrusted,
and I could not help suspecting when I heard the speech that
the ideas it contained, ideas which I had never heard him express
and which he himself seemed not fully to understand, had originated with some of the musical faddists he had met there. It was
in fact one of Edward's strangest peculiarities that while his
own work was based on so sound a musical instinct he would

nevertheless listen to the most utter nonsense talked by cranks
and would later solemnly repeat it with every sign of believing
it. But whatever the cause, this first lecture, with its high-
sounding enunciation of incomprehensible theories was one of
the most embarrassing failures to which it has ever been my
misfortune to listen. The opening was greeted with the respect-
ful attention which Edward's eminence deserved but as the
evening wore on and point after point missed its mark feet
were shuffled, a cross-fire of coughs set in and one gradually
realized that the day was hopelessly lost.

It should in justice be added that the storm of controversy
which surrounded these lectures has obscured the fact that some
of them were of considerable value. When Edward abandoned
what are believed to have been the theories picked up from his
friends and spoke simply of what he knew, he could often throw
a good deal of light on his subject.

The Elgars left for America on 19 June 1905 and the first
American trip proved to be one of his happiest holidays. He
was lucky too in his host, for Professor Sanford was a genial
tactful man who drew the best from him.

On 17 July the Elgars were back at Plas Gwyn but the dullness of the fizgigs was soon to be relieved by a shower of
engagements. On 5 September at Edward's invitation I attended
a rehearsal in London for the Three Choirs' Festival at which
Jaeger was present. He was back from Switzerland and a cure
which had all too obviously failed. It was on this occasion that
he begged me to try and separate Edward from some of his
newer friends.

Two days later Professor Sanford, who had come to England
for a holiday, gave a luncheon in Edward's honour at Pagani's.
The Professor was a witty and delightful host who knew how to
keep a large number of people entertained without apparent
effort and I soon understood why the American visit had been
so happy. The party stands out in my mind for one of those
surprising remarks with which Edward liked to administer

shock-therapy to his friends. Introducing me to Professor Sanford, he said, 'Without her I could not have written *Gerontius*'.
Dr Sanford, who was too well-bred to show surprise, bowed
and said he could believe it. But I, knowing Edward, guessed
that something more would follow. It was true that every passage in *Gerontius* had been tried and discussed at The Mount but
I did not expect any credit for the hours spent in that way; nor
did I get it.

'You see,' Edward added, 'she took Carice off our hands
while I was writing it.'

The Three Choirs' Festival was held that year in Worcester
which took occasion to present Edward with the freedom of
the city, an honour which must have been very gratifying to
old Mr Elgar who was able to see his son pass in the procession.
At the civic luncheon I was introduced to Mrs Worthington, one
of a number of new friends from America. No reference was
made this time to *Gerontius*. Instead I heard myself described as
'one of my intimate enemies'.

I think he enjoyed that festival. There was in him a very
natural desire to *épater le bourgeois* more especially the *bourgeois* of
the town in which he had spent an obscure youth. Now at last
he could appear in the gown of a foreign university, the lion of
a gay and brilliant company of friends and could bring with the
Introduction and Allegro, a masterpiece for performance not by
some local band of amateurs but by the London Symphony
Orchestra which now played at the Festivals.

The year 1906 was one of changes in both Edward's life and
mine. For him it meant the end of his oratorio-writing and for
me a complete break with Malvern. For both of us it ended a
period. The cycle-rides, the walks, the long discussions, though
interrupted by the Elgar's move to Hereford, had still been
possible at intervals. Now, for a time they were to end
altogether.

In the early months of 1906 I too had had a series of crushing troubles which, beginning with a disastrous series of epidemics at the school (hitherto free from such things), ended in something very like a nervous breakdown for myself. In a few short weeks I saw everything that I had built up collapse hopelessly and finally. I did not allow myself a nervous breakdown however. Realizing that the situation was quite hopeless, I closed the school and said good-bye to the children at the finish of the spring term, visited a few old friends and by the end of May had taken up an appointment in Portugal.

The wrench was the hardest I have ever had to face. The work of the school, the lovely Malvern countryside, the growth of Edward's fame, interests which had seemed to be part of the very texture of my life, all had to be torn out and left. Nor could I see, as I did many years later, that the change had been good for me. It dawned on me in the end that a headmistress, like any other dictator, is placed in a position of authority which almost inevitably turns her head, a position made dangerous moreover by the constant contact with immature minds. But at the time I was conscious only of the disaster and of the necessity of beginning a life in new surroundings.

It was the best anodyne I could have found. The past was not dead but I was cut off from its most painful consequences. And quite suddenly I realized that I was thankful for my freedom.

Henceforth for some years I was to watch Edward's career mainly from a distance but with occasional close-ups. Luckily he wrote me fairly regularly, and our friendship, although obviously not so close, was maintained for several years. Welcome though they were, those of his letters which have survived my travels contain little of general interest, and as this book is not intended to be either an autobiography or a biography of Elgar it seems best for the more or less continuous narrative to stop at this point. The following chapters therefore deal only with those periods or occasions when I was in close touch with the Elgars again.

23

The Violin Concerto and Second Symphony

In 1910 I was back in England and during the next twelve months I was to see a good deal of the Elgars as for much of that time we were all in England. Plas Gwyn was still their headquarters, and remained so until they moved to Hampstead at the beginning of 1912, but it was evident that Edward was tiring of Hereford and that he wanted to settle in London. The New Cavendish Street flat was taken for March, April and May of 1910 and a house in Gloucester Place (No. 75) for three months in the spring of 1911.

This restlessness was wholly typical and resulted from what I felt to be a disproportionate regard for the influence of environment. No matter where he was, Edward always seemed to imagine that he would be able to compose better somewhere else. Even the kind of weather favourable to composition did not seem to exist. Always it was too hot or too cold, too dry or too wet. This unhelpfulness of the weather—its lack of meteorological collaboration—was something of a grievance. To tell Edward, or even Alice, that rain was needed for the farmers was merely to add to the sense of injury because it showed a want of sympathy. The environmental fetish was equally offended when in the old days innocent visitors to Malvern complimented him on the beauty of his surroundings and said how easy it must be to compose music there. This always provoked him to a sort of dull rage and indeed his warmest appreciation of Malvern, as of every other place in which he lived, was not expressed until after he had left it.

Two major works were in hand when I arrived in London in 1910, the Violin Concerto and Second Symphony. When I first went to the flat I found that the concerto was the chief interest of the moment and that W. H. Reed of the London Symphony Orchestra was helping, somewhat as I had tried to help in earlier days with *Gerontius*, but with of course much greater skill, by playing over doubtful passages, testing the effect of counter-points and bowings and generally making himself musically useful. Mr Reed ultimately became one of Edward's most devoted and faithful friends. A simple and kindly soul, he may be said indeed to have taken the part in Edward's life of chief encourager formerly filled by Jaeger and we owe much to him beside the little piece *Sospiri* which was dedicated to him.

The Elgars had, I thought, been changed somewhat by Edward's now marked success. At our first meeting they seemed distant and aloof and showed a tendency which I thought rather ill-bred to refer at great length in the presence of a visitor to conversations which the visitor had not heard, with people whom he did not know. As our old relationship began to revive, however, these barriers, erected perhaps from a necessary habit of keeping the lion-hunters at bay, began to disappear.

Circumstances combined to prevent me from attending the first public performance of the concerto by Kreisler at the Royal Philharmonic Society's concert on 10 November, but I managed to hear the second performance which took place shortly afterwards, largely as a result of the success of the first.

The concerto had been dedicated to Kreisler. (One of the most hilarious of all Elgar misprints was made by a Worcester paper which announced that the concerto had been inscribed to Caruso, surely the very last dedicatee likely to be chosen by a composer who hated singers.) The name of the great violinist undoubtedly gave the work a useful send-off but its ultimate success showed that it needed no help of his and indeed Herr Kreisler seemed before long to have lost interest in it and to be quite willing to leave its performance to Albert Sammons and, much later, Yehudi Menuhin. It may well be that this coolness arose from a disagreement over performing fees, such as ultimately prevented Ysaye from playing the concerto in England.

Since 1905, when I had ceased to be actively concerned with what may be called Edward's workshop, I had never heard one of his new compositions without wondering what aspect of his character it would reveal and whether it would tell me anything new about him. The Violin Concerto is a long work, longer indeed than Brahm's First Symphony, but its emotional programme seemed to me simple and almost tragic. I noticed a few technical features, but it was the spirit of the concerto which impressed me most and which was to haunt me for many days.

There was much in the music that called up memories of days long past at Birchwood and Longdon, of rides through the sleepy Malvern country, but since these associations may have been largely subjective they are not worth mentioning in detail. What seemed to me universally obvious about the work was that it expressed a sadness of spirit such as Edward had rarely achieved before even in *Gerontius*. The sadness was exquisitely expressed, a very refinement of suffering indeed, but a suffering so acute and concentrated that one felt almost embarrassed by its intensity. Even the vigour of the last movement suggested the frenzy of despair rather than a solution of the emotional problem and it was not until after the cadenza that Edward seemed to be looking outward instead of contemplating his own sorrow.

The writing of the Violin Concerto did not exhaust Edward as that of his other big works had often done, partly perhaps because he was expressing in it a more direct and vividly realized emotion but partly, I think, because another work was clamouring for completion and had been simmering in his mind alongside the concerto. This was of course the Second Symphony to which he at once turned and which was com pleted at Plas Gwyn by the end of February 1911.

In the Spring he sailed for what was to be his last visit to America. This was less happy than the earlier ones had been, owing to some misunderstanding over a fee. Precisely what happened I do not know but, since his own countrymen had often unintentionally and unthinkingly insulted Edward by honouring him in every way but the rather necessary one of paying him for his services, it seems possible that his American admirers may have fallen into the same mistake. At any rate he returned to the house in Gloucester Place at the beginning of May in a chastened and, as it seemed to me, rather embittered frame of mind which a series of further irritations during the year did little to change.

The first of these arose in connection with the Coronation of King George V. Edward was now unquestionably the leading English composer and, either because he was asked to con tribute only an offertorium (*Oh Hearken Thou*) and a Coronation March or because the fee offered was inadequate, he felt aggrieved with results that were to be rather unfortunate. Then on 24 May the Second Symphony was given its first perform ance at the London Music Festival and fell completely flat. For the time being at any rate there seemed some justification for his habitual pessimism.

For me there has always been a certain amount of mystery about that first performance. The First Symphony and Violin Concerto had both made enormous successes and the Second Symphony, whatever its faults, is no less vital and vivid. One might therefore have supposed that it would achieve a similar welcome. A curious feature of the occasion was that the

audience was not only cool but extremely sparse, which seemed
to suggest that Edward was going through a phase of un-
popularity. Could it be that his exasperation over the Coronation commission had leaked out? That this exasperation was
very great is proved by the fact that, although he had been
invited to the Abbey for the ceremony, he refused to go or to
allow Alice to do so and this in spite of the fact that the honour
which he valued above all others, the Order of Merit, had been
conferred on him only five days earlier. Alice, whose devotion
was proof against almost any humiliation, was really hurt by
this prohibition.

Whatever the reason for the thin attendance and the luke-
warm reception, however, it was obvious to all who had ears
to hear that the Second Symphony was an enormous advance
on the First. At the first performance I sat with Alice whose
rather exaggerated appreciation of Edward's work, expressed
in sighs, shakings of the head and appealing looks, tended to
disturb one's own response to the music but I could not fail to
realize that this was an important achievement. Written at
almost the same time as the Violin Concerto, it seemed to me
the counterpart and compliment of the other work. Thus, while
the prevailing mood of the concerto had seemed to be one in
which suffering was accepted, and indeed almost enjoyed, that
of the symphony was very largely one of revolt, Edward's most
vigorous protest against the slings and arrows, a protest which
arose at times to something like a snarl. This it seemed to me
was far more healthy than the mood of the concerto and I
listened enthralled. Even the abrupt dismissal of the first movement with a conventional climbing phrase, though an unsatisfactory ending, seemed to fit the emotional programme of
the music. The moment that the orchestra began the last movement I found that my mind had been whisked back to the
holiday at Alassio over seven years earlier, to the memory of
twelve men delivering a small piano at the Villa San Giovanni
and of Edward's sitting down and playing the first tune that

came into his head. It was the same tune that the orchestra were now embroidering.

Whatever may be the faults of the Second Symphony, I have always found it a rich and splendid experience and in some strange way a vivid reminder of many facets of Edward's character. The Shelley lines, 'Rarely, rarely comest thou, Spirit of Delight' which he took as its motto might almost be the motto of his own life and there is in the opening phrase with its bold affirmation in bars 1 and 2 followed by the sudden collapse into sadness of bar 3 much that all who knew him must recognize as typical. When I first heard the symphony in May 1911 I had not attended an Elgar première for many years and the performance touched me so deeply that at first I hardly noticed the thinness of the applause or the coldness of the audience. It was all too soon apparent, however, and when Alice, who was deeply and justifiably hurt by it ('You should have heard them after the First Symphony and Violin Concerto, dear Rosa'), took me into the artists' room we found a very glum group of friends trying to console poor Edward. Among them were W. H. Reed who had led the orchestra (the London Symphony) and Ivor Atkins both of whom were assuring him of their belief in the greatness of the work. This belief was of course soon to be more than justified.

The Elgars left Gloucester Place, where they were living when the Second Symphony was first played, for Hereford towards the end of July, but before they went Edward took me one day up to Hampstead to see a house which had attracted him. It was a very impressive house standing half-way up the hill of Netherhall Gardens and as we walked through the empty rooms I saw that he meant, if it were financially possible—which I rather doubted—to live there. This was one of the strangest afternoons we ever spent together and I have never known the duality of his character so strongly marked as it was that day. On the one hand he clearly took a natural pride in the importance of the house with its fine panelling, its long music room and its great staircase at the head of which Alice would stand to receive her guests. But on the other hand he wanted equally clearly to make me feel that his success meant nothing to him and that there was always some lovely thing in life which had completely eluded him. As we explored the empty house he drew my attention to its beauties, but he also told me that the only part of his life that had ever been happy was the period of struggle at Malvern and that even now he never conducted his music without finding that his mind had slipped back to summer days on the Malvern Hills, to Birchwood or to the drowsy peace of Longdon Marsh.

24

Severn House and the War

The Elgars moved into their new home at Hampstead on 1 January 1912. Edward named it Severn House.

The place had originally been designed by Norman Shaw for a now forgotten painter named Edwin Long. The late nineteenth century was a profitable time for painters, especially bad painters, and the house was pretentious and handsome. It was also extremely inconvenient, utilitarian considerations such as comfortable bedrooms having been recklessly sacrificed to appearance. Its worst feature, however, was that it was a very expensive house for a composer—whose prosperity could never be expected to rival that of a painter of Academy pictures. And, although they managed to live there until 1920 when Alice's death necessitated a rearrangement of their finances, there is no doubt that Severn House was always something of an embarrassment.

It was, moreover, a house which, for all its luxury, never seemed to suggest happiness. There was a legend that the painter's widow used to sit, like the Greuze lady in the Wallace Collection, contemplating the bust of her husband and, although this was probably apocryphal, it did match the rather gloomy atmosphere of the rooms, an atmosphere which always seemed to drown any efforts at gaiety which the Elgars might make. There was thus the irony that, while they now at last had a home which was in harmony with Edward's position as leading English composer, they seemed unable to make use of the advantages it offered. The training and outlook of the Elgars were of course such as to make an unbuttoned mood very difficult for them except when they were strictly *en famille*, and the effect was a little chilling. Parties were given but their stiffness hardly ever relaxed into anything like joviality and the guests rarely felt wholly at ease. An odd feature was that music, which might have been expected to form the main attraction, was seldom heard on account of Edward's dislike of performers.

My return in 1912 after other spells abroad marked the beginning of a stay in England that lasted till 1920. During the end of 1912 I was mostly in London and saw much of the Elgars, finding Edward depressed and inclined to hypochondria, and Alice still as vague and unpractical as ever. A new friendship had been formed with Landon Ronald who was championing Edward's music at the time and whom Alice was inclined to regard as its finest interpreter. This was not a view with which I entirely agreed. Ronald was an accomplished musician and a professional conductor with a technique that Edward could never have commanded but I did not feel in Ronald's handling of the Second Symphony anything like the glow of sincerity, however clumsy the actual conducting, of Edward's own interpretation.

In general however I found that Edward's new friendships were with people unconnected with music which now he almost seemed to regard as an interest unworthy of serious attention. This pose, which puzzled some and exasperated others, was no doubt adopted for more reasons than one. It was still true in 1912 as it had been much earlier that he really practised the art of music and not of talking about it. It was also true that a composer of his eminence had every reason for being irritated by people who liked to air their own limited musical knowledge under the excuse of asking about technical details of his work. But I always suspected that the main reason for the non-musical pose was the conviction derived from early influences and deepened by contact with Alice's relatives and many of her friends, that music was not in reality a fitting concern for a man of the fashionable world.

Most of 1913 and 1914 I spent at Bayons Manor, Lincolnshire, with my friends the Tennyson D'Eyncourts. One of my chief enterprises there was the training of a village choir, a work in which Edward, who never practised his non-musical pose on me, gave me valuable and generous help with gifts of primers and advice. We won some prizes at competitions but as, in addition to Edward's support, I had that of Gervase Elwes who came over and sang at rehearsals with the men, it may be that we were at rather an unfair advantage.

If Edward's admirers had felt, as many must have done, that *The Crown of India* and *The Music Makers* showed signs of failing power, *Falstaff* instantly reassured them. As a mere piece of orchestral virtuosity it made an immediate impression at that first performance. Nikisch, who was present, warmly congratulated him and the applause was loud and long. What particularly delighted us was the essentially English quality of this music and the profoundly poetic feeling behind some of the passages such as the First Interlude. There were surprises of course. For one thing I had expected that Edward would take an opportunity of working off some of the emotions he had wanted to express years earlier in connection with Rabelais, but it was evident that those emotions had been swamped by either the respectability of Hampstead or the learning of the commentators he had consulted and the result was not exactly an essay in ribaldry. Then again I felt that the cohesion of the work depended less on its own structure than on the programme story to which it was attached, a view which has undoubtedly been shared by others. To this day it is necessary, if one is to follow all the details of this great work, 'to study the score,' as Dunhill says, 'side by side with each incident of the story it illustrates.' Few are in a position to do this and the necessity seems to imply a weakness. But the work we heard that night was a masterpiece and we knew it.

The effort of completing *Falstaff* had taken a good deal out of Edward and, either because he was nervy and expected too much deference or because of tactlessness on the part of the Leeds authorities, there had been the usual friction over his visit. As a result of his aesthetic exhaustion, he wrote nothing of importance during the rest of 1913 or indeed until well into 1914. *Carissima, Rosemary* and *Sospiri* date from this time but a more interesting work was the anthem *Give Unto the Lord* commissioned for the Festival of the Sons of the Clergy at St Paul's Cathedral. I rather think this had been in mind during the visit to Alassio when Dr Armitage Robinson had been asked to suggest a subject and had said with a vague wave of the arm 'Oh—Praise the Lord!'

I went to the first performance, for which we were given seats in the finely carved choir-stalls. Afterwards there was a party at Lady Martin's lovely old house near by but I am sorry to say that I remember almost nothing of the anthem except the beauty of the sound produced by the choir and orchestra and the peculiar quality of tone resulting from the acoustics of St Paul's Cathedral.

It was shortly after this that Henry Embleton, a wealthy supporter of the Leeds Choral Union, who had always had a strong personal affection for Edward, offered to commission the third part of the great oratorio trilogy for his choir. Edward was deeply stirred by this offer and went off to Gairloch in Sutherlandshire to consider it. Whether he could ever have overcome his increasing scepticism sufficiently to have carried out the task I do not know, but the oubreak of war on 2 August put an end to all such plans.

By 13 August, the Elgars were back at Severn House. I think it is true to say that people were stunned by the war of 1914, which broke upon what had seemed a relatively settled world, as they were not by that of 1939. At first one could see the great disaster only from a limited personal point of view and it meant that all our plans were suddenly frustrated. My own visit to Russia had to be cancelled at the last moment—unfortunately not until my luggage had gone, ultimately to be miraculously found at Hamburg nearly five years later—all concert engagements were wiped out, the future seemed darker and more terrible than anything artists had had to face within living memory. The Elgars, never given to over-optimism, were in the depths of despair when I called at Severn House on Friday, 24 August. On the following Sunday when I spent the day with them, things were no better.

Despite his military fantasies, Edward had little of the soldier in him but he rallied splendidly to the occasion, volunteered as a special constable and joined the Hampstead Volunteer Reserve.

'I am very busy with things that are in themselves slight,' he wrote to me on 30 September, 'but the assumption is that I am releasing a better man, which is pleasing.'

The first blow he had to face was the cancellation of the Three Choirs Festival, which should have taken place at Worcester that year, but many others followed. With great courage, however, he set to work to compose again and, although some of the songs he at first produced were of no great value, he soon turned out several works of considerable importance.

Like the rest of us, he had been deeply moved by the German invasion of Belgium and when he read Emile Cammaerts's stirring poem *Carillon* he at once decided to make a setting for it. But Edward's attempts at fitting words to music had never been very happy and had not grown happier with the passing of the years, as we had seen from *The Music Makers*. When, therefore, he told me of the project I ventured to suggest that he should not try to tie himself to the metre of the words, as he would have to do if the piece were treated as a song or a choral item, but that he should provide an illustrative prelude and entractes as background music for a recitation of the poem. This he did with immense success. A persistent four-note bell theme, which, as the music was in triple time, recurred with a constantly changing emphasis, served as the basis for music which, despite a heavy debt at one moment to Chopin's F major Ballade, enormously intensified the effect of the poem.

The first performance of the *Carillon* was given at Queen's Hall on 7 December and has remained in my memory for more reasons than one. Cammaerts's wife was the actress Tita Brand, whose mother Marie Brema had first sung the part of the Angel in *Gerontius* at Birmingham fourteen years earlier, and it seemed fitting that she should declaim her husband's poem. But unfortunately Mme Brand–Cammaerts was *enceinte* and in order to conceal this fact an enormous bank of roses was built on the platform over which her head and shoulders appeared rather in the manner of a Punch and Judy show. Mme Brand put such energy into the performance that both Edward, who was conducting the orchestra, and I, who was sitting in the audience, trembled for the effect on her, but patriotic fervour won the day and the *Carillon* was performed without mishap.

I was to see a good deal of the Elgars during the war years. The Christmas of 1914 I actually spent with them at Severn House and it was good to find that our old friendship, which had tended to cool during the long periods of separation, was becoming closer and warmer than it had been at any time since the old days at Malvern. When I arrived Alice was ill, having spent three weeks indoors, but Carice, who had come back from a holiday at Torquay, and Edward, who seemed to have recovered from the first shock caused by the war, and was in one of his facetious moods, were both well and cheerful.

For all his facetiousness there was no doubt that Edward had been deeply moved by the war or that some of the *pièces d'occasion* it inspired were more deeply felt and of greater value, if not of greater ultimate popularity, than some of his earlier essays in this direction. Early in 1915 he chanced on some war poems (*The Winnowing Fan*) by Laurence Binyon and was immediately fired to make choral settings of them. This resulted in something of a battle of courtesies for, on hearing that Dr Rootham of Cambridge was similarly engaged with them, Edward decided to abandon the project. In the end, however, it was Dr Rootham who gave in. I do not know why we were not allowed a setting by each composer. *The Fourth of August*, *To Women* and *For the Fallen*, composed separately, were ultimately grouped together under the title, *The Spirit of England*, the first performance of the complete work being given on 26 March 1917. This was an almost harrowing experience and I remember that Gervase Elwes, who had taken part, told me that he hardly knew how they had all got through it. The war casualties at that time were heartrending and almost every member of the choir must have lost a close relative or a friend.

It does not seem to be generally known that this work was written largely in Sussex. When the war prevented my visit to Russia I had gone to live for a time with Admiral and Mrs Caulfeild at their beautiful old house, Hookland, in West Sussex. In the summer of 1915 we all left for a holiday and the Caulfeilds offered Hookland to the Elgars for a few weeks. They accepted and the change did Edward good.

His relations with the Caulfeilds brought out a charming facet of Edward's character very different from either the morbidity or the facetiousness one knew too well. He was not a man who could be said to be fond of children but the beauty and charming manners of the young Caulfeilds, who greatly admired his music and whom he first met early in 1915, won his friendship and affection from the start.

25

Finale

The beauty of West Sussex had made a deep impression on Edward and in the May of 1917, tired and rather dispirited, he managed to find at Fittleworth, in the same neighbourhood as Hookland, a cottage to which he and Alice could retire when they felt oppressed by Severn House. Brinkwells also had belonged to an artist and its amenities included a separate studio in the garden which could be used as a music room. The views over stretches of Sussex woodland were magnificent.

The impulse to compose anything but trifles seemed almost to have left Edward in 1916 and the early part of 1917, but the stimulus of new and beautiful surroundings had its effect and new ideas at once began to germinate. For the moment, however, he was too occupied with engagements to conduct *The Fringes* and he was back at Severn House in June.

He managed to snatch a few odd days at Brinkwells later in the year but the engagement list was heavy and, until Kipling vetoed further performances of the song-cycle, there were visits to pay all over the Midlands. But he was still ailing.

'. . . I am not so well internally,' he writes in January 1918, 'I suffer much. All good wishes for 1918.' Finally he had his tonsils removed.

It was while he was in the nursing home in Dorset Square that thoughts of Brinkwells inspired the beginnings of a string quartet. This was quickly followed by plans for a sonata for violin and piano and a quintet.

The 'Cello Concerto was not finished during 1918 and in fact was to provide the chief musical occupation for the spring and summer of 1919 at Brinkwells. But the three chamber-works were all ready early in the New Year and were given a trial performance, or rather, I think, a series of trial perform-ances, before friends in the big music-room at Severn House. On 7 March, when I heard them, the party included Bernard Shaw, for whom in later years Edward had conceived a great admiration, and the music was played by William Murdoch, Albert Sammons, W. H. Reed, Raymond Jeremy and Felix Salmond, a distinguished ensemble indeed. The same artists, strengthened by the co-operation of Landon Ronald, who played the pianoforte part in the sonata, gave the first public performance of the three works at the Aeolian Hall a fortnight later.

The year 1920 marks the point at which this history ends. In that year a period of Edward's life was closed and he had hence-forth to face an almost entirely different existence. Although he was only 63, his work as a composer was virtually finished; the heavy taxation following the war was making the maintenance of Severn House impossible and public taste in music was turn-ing towards austerer ideals than his. But the most serious change was one in his domestic life.

Early in 1920 I spent a day at Severn House and was shocked to find Alice shrunken and terribly depressed. She seemed to rally, however, for a time and to take an interest in the many honours which were being poured on to Edward and in the all-Elgar concert which Landon Ronald conducted at Queens Hall. But it was only a temporary revival, the concert was the last she attended and on 7 April she suddenly died.

There is no doubt that her death after thirty-one years of their married life came as an overwhelming blow to him but it was not in reality precisely the kind of blow which has been described by most of his biographers.

'Only those who knew the Elgars in their family life are

competent to estimate the value or extent of' (her) 'influence,'
wrote Dunhill. And unfortunately the only biographer who
did so know the Elgars (other than Miss Dora Penny, to whom
they do not seem to have confided their deeper discontents)
was W. H. Reed who was too blindly devoted to his hero not
to distort the facts in that hero's favour.

That Alice had devoted her whole life to Edward is beyond
question. She really did worship him with a blindness to his
faults, and indeed to his occasional cruelty to her, that seemed
almost incredible. But it is equally true that, while relying on
this devotion, he was in the first place rather impatient of its
blindness and in the second uncomfortably guilty over his debt
to it. Her death accentuated the conflict in his soul and left him
completely stunned. He had not the largeness of mind which
enabled Disraeli to overlook the faults of understanding of the
woman whose fortune had established him. The marriage had
been in many ways irksome and irritating. Many of the friends
whose wealth had dazzled Edward in the later years had barely
concealed their contempt for Alice, but Alice's extremely conventional standards of correct conduct had already made an
indelible impression on him and throughout his life he had been
at immense pains to maintain a façade of married bliss.

So stunned was he by the blow, so withdrawn into himself
that no one at Severn House dared to approach him even when
the undertaker had to be interviewed. I was in the house at the
time and, realizing that something had to be done, I went into
the study and told him as gently as I could that he really must
pull himself together.

That he put the insignia of his honours into the coffin saying
that he had only accepted them to please her is well known.
The action was bitterly criticized and indeed, whatever they
may say, men do not actually accept honours merely to please
their wives, but I think Edward was sincere in feeling that by
this act he was paying some small part of a heavy debt.

She was buried in the hillside grave at Little Malvern where

Edward also now lies. W. H. Reed, always the gentlest and
most considerate of men, took down his quartet party to the
service at St Wulstan's where, at the request of Carice, they
played the slow movement, which Alice had particularly loved,
of Edward's String Quartet.

I have few memories of Edward after this point. Shortly
after Alice's death I took an appointment in Prague and for a
time saw very little of him. When I ultimately returned to
England I found that I was one of a number of friends who had
been tacitly dropped though I am glad to say that Carice has
remained my friend to this day. It was odd after nearly thirty
years of intimate friendship to meet him face to face as often
happened at festivals and to find that I was completely ignored,
nor do I know why our friendship ended as no word of
explanation was ever offered even when it was asked for. I can
only guess that an overmastering sense of guilt towards Alice
led him to shun the society of those who had been allowed to
look behind the façade of happiness and who were thus regarded
as having in some measure connived in his disloyalty to her.

Two further facts may be recorded, however, for the light
they shed on his very curious character.

In 1932 the Three Choirs Festival was held in Worcester
where Edward, after occupying various houses in the district,
had settled in what was to prove his last home. That year no
less than six of his works had been included in the Festival
programme yet he could actually bring himself to say at a tea-
party that since no one wanted his music nowadays it was useless for him to complete the score of his Third Symphony
although it was actually written.

For once he had overstepped the mark. The news quickly
leaked out; the *Daily Mail* demanded a hearing for the
symphony; Sir Landon Ronald approached Sir John Reith of
the B.B.C. and a contract was immediately forthcoming for
delivery of the score of the symphony with payment in advance.
'The offer,' says Colles in *Grove's Dictionary* 'was to prove

embarrassing. The symphony was no more really written than were the third oratorio and the opera.' The fact is that Edward's ineradicable self-pity had led him to make a statement so completely untrue as utterly to defeat its own ends.

He made a gallant effort to write the symphony but his health and his power of concentration had gone. All that could be handed to the B.B.C. after his death was a chaotic pile of manuscript which he himself besought W. H. Reed to allow no one to sort out or attempt to put into shape.

The other fact is less striking but no less curious. At the Christmas of 1932 a few months after the boast described above, I was surprised to receive a card from him. It had been posted in the Earl's Court district and was inscribed simply, 'From Edward'. As he had resolutely cut me for many years and as even our years of friendship had brought me a good deal of pain, I was careful in writing a letter of thanks to indicate as gently as possible that I did not wish to resume our past relationship. But I was rather puzzled by this sudden mark of recognition and wondered why it had been made. Could it be that he hoped by reviving an old friendship to recapture some of the youthful urge towards composition of past years? I shall never know.

Index of Works by Elgar

General Index

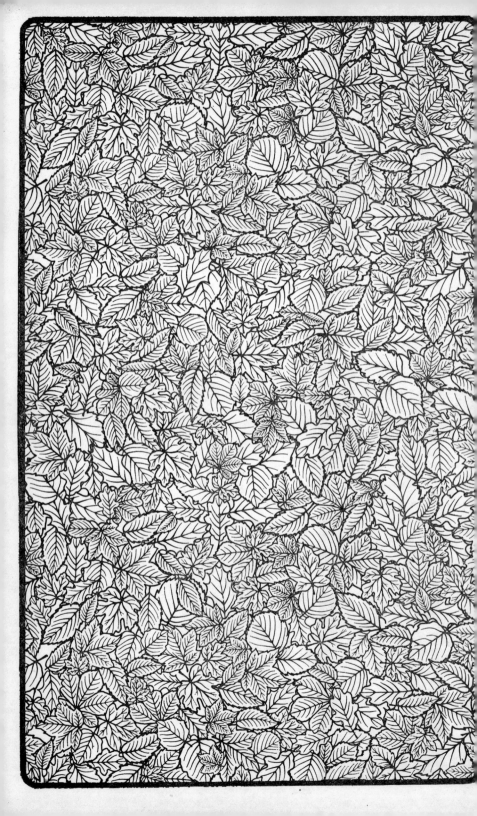